Can They Do That?

CAN THEY DO THAT?

A Guide to Your Rights on the Job

Michael A. Zigarelli

LEXINGTON BOOKS
An Imprint of Macmillan, Inc.
NEW YORK

Maxwell Macmillan Canada
TORONTO

Maxwell Macmillan International
NEW YORK   OXFORD   SINGAPORE   SYDNEY

Library of Congress Cataloging-in-Publication Data

Zigarelli, Michael A.
Can they do that? : a guide to your rights on the job /
Michael A. Zigarelli.
p.   cm.
Includes index.
ISBN 0-02-935823-X
1. Employee rights—United States—Popular works.
2. Labor laws and legislation—United States—Popular works.
I. Title.
KF3319.6.Z54   1994
344.73'01—dc20
[347.3041]   94-13199
CIP

Lexington Books
An Imprint of Macmillan, Inc.
866 Third Avenue, New York, N.Y. 10022

Maxwell Macmillan Canada, Inc.
1200 Eglinton Avenue East
Suite 200
Don Mills, Ontario M3C 3N1

Macmillan, Inc. is part of the Maxwell Communication Group of Companies.

Printed in the United States of America

printing number
1   2   3   4   5   6   7   8   9   10

2

To my father, Michael J. Zigarelli, whose years of dedicated service in the construction industry taught me to respect American workers, and to my mother, Alberta M. Zigarelli, whose selfless and giving nature has inspired me to assist them.

I would also like to acknowledge those who reviewed earlier drafts of this book for style, readability, and accuracy. I extend my thanks to Michael and Kathleen Pregitzer, to Patrick C. Cummings, and especially to my editor Beth Anderson, her assistant Jennifer Shulman, and an anonymous outside reviewer. Your insights and constructive suggestions have greatly improved the quality of this book and are sincerely appreciated.

Contents

WAGES AND HOURS

BENEFITS

EMPLOYEE SAFETY AND HEALTH

Introduction

So this is a book about employment law. Well, forget the complex legal terms. Spare me the ten-dollar words. I just want to know what my rights are!

S o do a lot of people. Recently, a friend asked me if he had to submit to his company's policy of annual employee drug testing. Two weeks earlier a relative wanted information on what constitutes sexual harassment. More and more, the answers to these types of questions are being sought by employees, people just like you, who are increasingly concerned about their job rights and their job security.

As you're well aware, the list of suspicious and frustrating practices that occur at work is endless: the copy machine is emitting something that makes you sick to your stomach; a manager searches your locker, desk, or computer files without your permission; a recent memo about your 401(k) plan makes you wish you had paid more attention in algebra class. Workers today need simple but complete answers to questions about their employment rights. And managers need to understand the law to keep from making mistakes that will land them and their companies in court.

If you're not a lawyer, this book is written for you. It covers all aspects of employment law in *plain English*—no Latin terms, no case law citations, no footnotes, no fifty-word sentences or long-winded explanations. Just concise information that has practical applications to your everyday work life.

The material is organized into sections that deal with discrimination and discharge, employee privacy, wages and hours, benefits, and worker safety and health. A glance at the table of contents will reveal that most of these sections have many chapters. That's because the chapters are short in length and narrow in focus: each chapter deals with a separate issue so you'll have an easier time finding what you're looking for and understanding what you find.

Although this book is designed to be a quick-reference handbook, to be used over and over again when you need it, it can also be read from cover to cover by those seeking a general awareness of the protection that the law affords them. In fact, it's probably a good idea to read the book through once just so you'll be prepared. While this book won't make you a lawyer, it should make you aware of all kinds of rights you never knew you had.

By the way, don't be surprised if you find that something your employer is doing violates the law. Chances are this violation is not even intentional. Employment law is so vast and complex that even the boss doesn't know all the rules (actually, some may not know *any* of the rules). Having a general knowledge of the law, then, should make you a valuable asset to both your coworkers and your boss.

Where the Laws Come From

Before looking up any issue, it's helpful to recognize that your employment rights come from several places: from statutes (federal and state laws), from local ordinances (city, town, or county laws), from common law (law made by judges), and sometimes from the U.S. and state Constitutions and government agency regulations. All of it, taken together, is what we call employment law. You certainly don't need to memorize this information to understand the chapters in this book, but you should remember the following: **on some issues, you are protected by more than** one law. **If those laws conflict, you can rely on the one that gives you greater rights.**

For example, there is a federal law that entitles you to twelve weeks of unpaid family leave. Your state may have a family leave law but it may entitle you to only six weeks of leave. Because the federal law gives you greater rights, that is the one you rely on to resolve the conflict. You get twelve weeks of leave. However, if your state law said that you could receive six weeks of paid leave and six more weeks of unpaid leave, the state law would give you the greater rights. In this case, it is the state law that your employer would have to obey.

To minimize the confusion of conflicting laws, after detailing the boundaries of the federal law on any issue, many chapters provide a table of the state laws or other laws that grant you greater protections than do the federal laws. As you'll see, this system should make it relatively simple to determine which law applies to you.

One final note before you begin. Employment laws change, sometimes rapidly. Although most laws covered in this book will remain pretty much the same for years to come, some will change. For example, the minimum wage may rise, there could be changes in the law concerning an employer's ability to replace strikers, occupational safety and health standards may become tighter, there may be adjustments in Social Security and unemployment compensation rules, and employers may be required to provide health insurance for employees. The central goal in this book is to provide you with accurate information about your employment rights, but be warned: any resource on the law will become somewhat outdated over time. So here's one important piece of advice: the longer you own this book, the more important it will be to double check whatever information you're looking up. To do this, call the appropriate government agency. Their phone numbers are listed in Appendix A.

Can They Do That?

1

Can They Ask Me That During an Interview?

The interviewer smiled as he proceeded to the next question. "So Mary," he said cheerfully, "I see from that ring that you're married. Do you have any children?" Mary, who did indeed have two young boys, knew that if she answered truthfully, she probably wouldn't get the job. And if she refused to answer what she thought might be an illegal question, they'd find some other reason to deny her employment.

We all know that job interviewers cannot ask you certain questions. Inquiries about your race and ethnic background, your religious beliefs, your age, and your dependents strike most of us as irrelevant and probably unlawful. But the legality of questions about your political affiliation, your arrest record, and your height and weight is less obvious. Just what are the boundaries of an employment interview and what rights do you have during such an interview?

What Can't They Ask?

As you will learn from the chapters that follow, the **Civil Rights Act of 1964 (Title VII)** and several other statutes outlaw discrimination against job applicants and employees. With regard to hiring, Title VII makes it unlawful to consider an applicant's race, color, gender, religion, or national origin in the hiring decision. Moreover, Title VII makes it unlawful *to even ask about* these characteristics on the job application or during an interview.

Why can't an employer ask about these characteristics? The reasoning is logical and simple: if an employer's job application asks questions about the applicant's race or national origin, certain minority groups may be discouraged from applying because they will anticipate discriminatory treatment. Even though the employer may not have intended to discriminate against anyone, the mere existence of such questions may affect who applies in the first place, and could screen out minorities in greater numbers. To prevent such a situation, the employer is typically barred from asking applicants or employees about their race, color, gender, religion, or national origin.

Thanks to other federal laws, the same is true for questions about your age and disabilities. Additionally, some states prohibit preemployment questions about marital status, sexual orientation, smoking, parenthood, and other things not considered relevant to your job performance.

What all this regulation means for employers is that they must be very careful about what they ask. Even simple questions like "When did you graduate from high school?" Or "Is it *Mrs.* or *Miss* Cummings?" could open the door to a discrimination suit based on age or marital status. The smart employer will therefore avoid directly seeking information about anything that isn't related to your ability to do the job.

What, then, are the ground rules for an interview? Table 1.1 summarizes the legality of many interview questions, and Table 1.2 presents information about additional protections you might have in your state.

Summary

By now, most employers have gotten the message that they're taking a pretty big risk if they seek information about you that has little to do with your ability to do a job. Therefore, it's

TABLE 1.1

The Legality of Interview Questions

Questions About:	Generally Legal?	Exceptions
Your name	YES	You shouldn't be asked about your maiden name or any previous names (marital status or national origin discrimination)
		Applications should not require you to denote "Mr., Mrs., Miss, Ms." (marital status or gender discrimination)
Your residence	YES	You shouldn't be asked whether you rent or own (singles out minorities in greater numbers)
Your race or color	NO	You may be asked to fill out a form for affirmative action purposes, but this is strictly voluntary—you are not *required* to do so
Your gender, religion, or national origin	NO	There are only a few jobs where it is legal to consider applicants from only one gender, religious group, or national origin. This is explained in chapter 3.
		Some religions do not permit work on certain days. An employer is allowed to ask you about your availability to work on weekends or if you have any problems with the hours of the job.
Pregnancy, number of children, child-rearing plans	NO	
Age	NO	You can be asked whether you meet the minimum age requirements for the state in which you'd be working
Citizenship, birthplace	NO	You will be asked to verify that you are eligible to work in the United States (Form I-9)

TABLE 1.1 (Continued)

Questions About:	Generally Legal?	Exceptions
Health, disability	NO	You can be asked if there are any reasons you would not be able to perform the job.
		You can usually be tested for drugs before being offered a job
		After you have been offered the job, the employer can require a medical exam and can inquire about your disabilities, about previous workers' compensation claims, and about your general health
Your sexual orientation	YES	There are nine states and several cities where an employer is not permitted to ask you about your sexual preference (see table 1.2)
Your work experience, skills, former employers, reasons for leaving your jobs, and dates of employment	YES	
Your education	YES	You should not be asked your dates of attendance of any schools (age discrimination)
		You should not be asked about education if education is not relevant to the job (because this may dispro-portionately screen out minorities)
Employer references	YES	
Union affiliation	NO	
Affiliation with other social groups	NO	You may be asked if you are a member of a professional, trade, or technical organization if it is relevant to the job
Language ability	NO	You may be asked about this if facility with a certain language is a requirement of the job

TABLE 1.1 *(Continued)*

Questions About:	Generally Legal?	Exceptions
Arrest record	NO	
Criminal convictions	YES	You shouldn't be asked about convictions if the information is not relevant to the job
Personal finances	NO	
Photographs, eye color, hair color	NO	
Military experience	NO	You may be asked about relevant skills that you acquired in the military You may be asked if you would voluntarily like to identify yourself as a military veteran for affirmative action purposes

unlikely that you'll encounter any questions as blatant as the one Mary was asked in the opening scenario. But watch out. Employers know plenty of sneaky tricks that they commonly use to obtain personal information. An interviewer might begin the interview by making small talk about his or her family, or about how tough it is to get a babysitter, thereby inviting you to discuss your situation. Or a secretary may inquire about which health insurance option, individual or a family plan, you'd like to select if you are hired, thereby allowing the interviewer to estimate how much you would cost the employer in health benefits. Be polite, but don't fall into such traps. As a rule of thumb, try to avoid providing any personal information until *after* employer has formally offered you a job.

TABLE 1.2
Special State Prohibitions

Most states make it illegal to ask questions about an applicant's race, color, gender, national origin, religion, age, or disabilities. The states listed below prohibit other types of discrimination and make it unlawful to ask about the following:

Marital status	Alaska, California, Connecticut, District of Columbia, Florida, Hawaii, Illinois, Iowa, Kansas, Maine, Maryland, Massachusetts, Michigan, Minnesota, Montana, Nebraska, New Hampshire, New Jersey, New Mexico, New York, North Dakota, Oregon, Virginia, Washington, Wisconsin
Sexual orientation	California, Connecticut, District of Columbia, Hawaii, New Jersey, Minnesota, Massachusetts, Oregon, Vermont, Wisconsin (and about 130 cities and municipalities)
Smoking habits	Colorado, Connecticut, Illinois, Indiana, Kentucky, Louisiana, Maine, Mississippi Nevada, New Hampshire, New Jersey, New Mexico, North Dakota, Oklahoma, Oregon, Rhode Island, South Carolina, South Dakota, Tennessee, Virginia
Arrest record	California, Hawaii, Illinois, Oregon (expunged juvenile record), Rhode Island, Wisconsin
Conviction record	Hawaii, Wisconsin
Parenthood/ family obligations	Alaska, Connecticut, District of Columbia
Use of birth control	Connecticut
Welfare status	Minnesota, North Dakota
Personal appearance	District of Columbia
Political affiliation	District of Columbia, California
Height and weight	Michigan

DISCRIMINATION
AND
DISCHARGE

2

An Overview of Discrimination Law and Wrongful Discharge

True story: A restaurant manager suspected that one of his waitresses was stealing from the company but could not identify the guilty party. He called the waitresses together for a meeting and told them that if someone did not confess, he'd begin firing them in alphabetical order. When no one came forward, he fired the first waitress on the list.

Clearly illegal, right? She can sue and get her job back, right? Actually, it depends. We'd like to think that any arbitrary treatment at the hands of our employer would be illegal, but that's not really the case. In truth, employer decisions concerning hiring, training, compensation, promotion, transfer, layoff, and termination are legal unless some law or court case says that they are not. In other words, employers are free to operate as they please unless their behavior has been forbidden by a legislative body or by a judge.

A few illustrations should clarify this point. Let's say a company decides to fire you because of your race. Because we have several laws that prohibit such conduct, the decision is illegal. If, on the other hand, the company decides to fire you because you are gay, is *that* illegal? In some areas of the country the answer is "yes," but in other areas it is "no."

Why the disparity? Simply because some places have specifically prohibited discrimination based on sexual orientation whereas others have not. Where the law and the courts are silent on the issue of sexual orientation discrimination, it's generally permitted.

Employment at Will

The legal concept that underlies the employer's freedom to act is called **"employment at will."** In simplest terms, this means that you can be fired for a good reason, for a bad reason, or for no reason at all. Pretty harsh stuff. The flip side, though, is that you are free to quit at *any* time and for *any* reason.

Employment at will is at the core of most of our employer-employee relationships in the United States. However, through legislation, court decisions and union contracts we've modified this condition considerably.

For example, a hundred years ago I could fire someone just because she was female. Why? The employment at will rule allowed me to. Now, in a more enlightened era, I can't do this because we've outlawed gender discrimination. The law, in essence, has restricted a piece of employment at will.

In fact, it's restricted *many* pieces. It's now unlawful to discriminate on the basis of race, color, gender, religion, national origin, pregnancy, age, disability, and—in some places—marital status, arrest record, or sexual orientation. Federal discrimination laws, written by Congress, have made most of these practices illegal *everywhere* in the country, while state laws and local government ordinances prohibit others within their own jurisdiction. The next four chapters will cover the specifics of discrimination cases.

Wrongful Discharge Cases

Written laws do not cover every possible type of unfair treatment you might encounter. Occasionally, scenarios develop (like the one that opened this chapter) that no legislative body has ever thought to address. To fill this void, judges sometimes provide another avenue, called common law, that will enable employees to overcome unjust employer decisions. Common law differs from federal and state laws in that no legislative process produces it. It is simply created through a judge's ruling in a case. That ruling thereafter has the same effect as any statute within the judge's jurisdiction.

Why would judges do this? Usually because they believe that it is the fair thing to do. Common law allows judges to fill in the gaps when statutes don't cover every possible contingency. This type of case is usually referred to as a **"wrongful discharge"** case.

Let's say, for instance, that you tell your boss that you need time off to serve jury duty. The boss, being somewhat less civic-minded than you, says no. When you insist that you *must* serve, the boss fires you, believing that he has the power under the employment at will rule to act in this manner.

To get your job back, you seek some federal or state statute that says the boss can't do this. To your chagrin, though, you find plenty of laws protecting you from termination based on gender, race, and other things referenced above, but no law specifically protecting you from termination because you have jury duty. Case dismissed? Not exactly. In many states, despite the lack of a specific jury duty statute, judges have ruled that it's illegal to fire an employee who must serve on a jury. It's not fair to the employee and it hurts our nation's ability to promptly seat juries. It's a wrongful discharge in the eyes of the court. The judge's opinion becomes law—a common law—that says one cannot be fired for serving jury duty. This and other common law exceptions to employment at will are discussed in chapter 7.

Union Contracts

Besides using discrimination laws and common law, workers can also protect themselves from pure at-will status through unionization. Unions secure contracts that, among other things, prevent the employer from firing without a good reason. The employer is therefore contractually prohibited from arbitrarily dismissing employees. This strongest protection from the employment at will rule is addressed in chapter 8.

Summary

In a nutshell, then, it all boils down to this: you can be fired for goofing off, for incompetence, for being late, and for a thousand other reasons as well. You probably already knew that. What you may not have known is that discrimination law and common law provide you with substantial protections from unfair or discriminatory treatment in all aspects of your employment. The next few chapters detail the boundaries of those protections.

3

Discrimination Based on Race, Color, Sex, Religion, or National Origin

The new owners walked into the reception area for the first time and took a look around. Olivia, a black woman who had competently handled the receptionist's job for several years, greeted them with a cheerful "Good morning, gentlemen!" Barely acknowledging her remark, one turned to the other and said, "You know. It's a bit too colorful in here. The new clients won't like that. Perhaps a more traditional look would be better." A few days later Olivia was fired and replaced with an inexperienced white woman.

As outrageous as this sounds, once upon a time this type of action was perfectly legal. Workers had no laws to protect them from discrimination. There wasn't a court in the country that would call Olivia's termination illegal.

Thankfully, things are different today. For many reasons, almost *every* court would now find this kind of action illegal. The most important of these reasons is the **Civil Rights Act of 1964 (Title VII)** which outlaws workplace discrimination on the basis of race, color, sex, religion, and national origin.

Passed at the height of the civil rights movement, Title VII is a far-reaching federal law that applies to all employers with fifteen or more employees (employers with fewer than fifteen employees are usually subject to state laws that parallel the Title VII protections), to labor unions, and to employment agencies. It is no understatement to say that in the thirty years since its adoption, Title VII has substantially altered almost every aspect of the employer–employee relation.

Every hiring, discipline, and termination decision is policed by Title VII. Every pay, training, transfer, and promotion decision must conform to the boundaries that Title VII sets. In short, this law has forever changed the rules of the game in American business.

The Two Types of Discrimination

There are two types of discrimination: that which intentionally targets an individual or group, and that which harms a group regardless of the employer's intentions.

The first type is easy to grasp. I refuse to give you a job because you're black. Or I fire you because you're pregnant and every other woman who becomes pregnant. Where an employer intentionally treats an individual differently because of his or her race, color, sex, religion, or national origin, the employer violates Title VII. This is called **"disparate treatment"** by lawyers and the courts. "Disparate" simply means different.

The second type of discrimination does not have to be intentional. Let's say I like blue-eyed people. I believe them to be more trustworthy. In fact, I have so much faith in the trustworthiness of blue-eyed people that I will not give a job to anyone who does not have blue eyes. Even though I haven't intended to discriminate against anyone, I've just succeeded in eliminating the entire black race from consideration for a job. My policy has a **"disparate impact"** on a group that is protected by Title VII, so the policy may be illegal.

A more realistic example is this: I will not hire anyone for a firefighter's position unless that individual can carry a two-hundred-pound dummy for one hundred yards while wearing complete firefighting gear. On the face of it, this policy is neutral. It doesn't seek to discriminate against any individual.

However, fewer women than men will be able to meet this standard; therefore, it has a disparate impact on female applicants.

As we'll see, a policy that has a disparate *impact* is not automatically illegal. Employers who have a good reason for a policy can often successfully defend it. An employer who is clearly guilty of disparate *treatment*, though, will seldom prevail.

Proving a Disparate Treatment Case

There are three steps involved in these cases. In step 1, you have to show the court that you meet some initial requirements. If you were *denied employment* for a discriminatory reason, you must show that:

1. you are a member of a group protected by Title VII,
2. you applied for and were qualified for the job.
3. you were denied employment, and
4. after the rejection, the employer continued to seek applicants.

However, if you were *fired or disciplined* for a discriminatory reason, as in the case of Olivia, your initial requirements are to show that:

1. you are a member of a group protected by Title VII, and
2. you were discharged (or disciplined) while a person outside of your protected group who had equal or lesser qualifications was retained or hired for your position.

After you overcome this first hurdle, it's the employer's turn. Step 2 requires the employer to give the court a legitimate, nondiscriminatory reason for its action. If you didn't get hired, the employer must tell the court why. Similarly, if you were fired, the employer better have a good reason for terminating your employment.

Once the employer presents its justification for its actions, the burden falls squarely on your shoulders to prove not only that the reason the employer gave is not true, but also that the employer *intended to discriminate against you*. This isn't an easy thing to do since there's seldom concrete evidence of this fact. Although Congress may amend this third step in the near future, currently you are faced with the heavy burden of proving discriminatory intent.

So returning to Olivia's discharge for a moment, because she's in a protected group (blacks), because she was discharged, and because she was replaced by a person from outside her protected group who was less qualified, she passes step 1. In step 2 the employer would probably contend something like it needed to cut costs by hiring someone who would work for a lot less money. In other words, it would attempt to present a legitimate reason for Olivia's discharge. In step 3, Olivia must prove that the employer really intended to discriminate against her. As concrete evidence, she could recount the conversation in the reception area, for instance, and the new owner's references to color, tradition, and client preferences. She could also raise the issue of timing: her dismissal came shortly after this conversation. If other blacks were fired at the same time, that would be important supporting evidence too.

Suspicious? Yes. Proof of disparate treatment? That really depends on whom the court or jury believes and on all of the evidence presented. Maybe the owners actually did seek to cut costs. Maybe they did remodel the reception area. Or, maybe Olivia's attorney got one of them to contradict himself or admit to the wrongdoing while on the witness stand. As strong as Olivia's case may seem to us, she may not prevail, for these cases are often quite difficult to win.

Proving a Disparate Impact Case

Disparate impact cases involve employer practices that have a tendency to discriminate against some protected group. *Whether the employer actually intended to discriminate is irrelevant.*

As with disparate treatment, there are three steps to proving a case. Step 1 requires you to produce evidence that suggests that discrimination indeed existed. However, the nature of that evidence is very different from evidence in disparate treatment cases. In step 1, you have to present specific proof that the employer's practice (or practices) limited the employment opportunities of a protected class. Using the firefighters example, there are two ways to do this. First, you can compare the percentage of women in the city to the percentage of women employed by the fire department. This may imply that the employer's hiring criteria have discriminatory results.

A second method is called the "four-fifths rule." In regard to the results of the dummy-carrying test, if the passing rate for women is less than four-fifths the passing rate for men, the court will consider the employer's test suspicious. In other words, if 30 percent of the female applicants and 50 percent of the male applicants pass this test, the ratio of the rates of women to men is 30 to 50, or three-fifths. The passing rate for women is three-fifths the rate for men. Since that's less than four-fifths, the court will presume that there is discrimination unless the employer can prove otherwise.

So for step 1, if you can demonstrate that there's a significant imbalance in the employer's workforce, or that the employer's policy does not meet the four-fifths rule, you will prompt the court to move on to step 2.

In step 2 the employer must prove that the test or policy in question is "job-related" and exists only because it's necessary for the business. The city or town government (the firefighters' employer) would likely argue that the job sometimes requires firefighters to carry adults long distances out of burning buildings. The test simulates real job conditions and is therefore job-related. If the city or town cannot convince the court that the test is necessary for the job and that it indeed tests a person's ability to carry adults, the case is over and the city or town will be ordered to find other tests that don't discriminate against women. If the city is successful in persuading the court, you will have to contend with step 3.

In step 3 you must prove either that the employer adopted the test specifically to discriminate against women *or* that there's some other test that serves the same interest of the employer, but has less of an impact on women's employment opportunities.

Either way, your task will be difficult. In this example, the task may be impossible. In that event, the employer would win and the test would remain.

Refusing to Hire Individuals in a Protected Group

There's one more way that employers can justify discriminating against you. The law recognizes that some jobs in society may be inappropriate for a particular group of people (because of their sex, for instance). Before you go ballistic, hear me out.

Before 1970, Pan American Airways limited flight attendant positions to women because it claimed customers preferred them. When the policy was challenged in court by a man, Pan Am lost a sex discrimination suit. Johnson Controls, a company that makes batteries, prevented fertile women from taking jobs that exposed them to lead. This policy was nullified by the court as well. But when the state of Alabama told women that they couldn't be employed as prison guards in an all-male penitentiary, the court permitted it.

In all of these cases, an employer contended that only one sex could do the job without hurting the business. Courts will seldom accept such logic, and do so only if they find that compelling the employer to hire both sexes for a position will truly jeopardize the essence of the business. In the prison guard case, for example, Alabama successfully argued that (1) because prisons contained large numbers of sex offenders, (2) because incarcerated offenders had been deprived of normal heterosexual activity, and (3) hiring female guards for male prison would lead to rapes, assaults, and more problems controlling the inmate population. The court agreed that a woman's ability to maintain order in a male prison was reduced simply because she was a woman. Therefore, the court upheld the state's employment policy. But remember, such cases are rare because there are few jobs where hiring one sex will severely hurt the business.

This defense (for the record, it's called a Bona Fide Occupational Qualification, or BFOQ) may also apply in some cases of religious, national origin, or age discrimination. A Catholic school might be permitted to reserve its religious education teaching positions for Catholics. A Japanese steak house could probably successfully argue that hiring an Irish waiter detracts from its authenticity. A bus company or an airline can usually limit its driver or pilot positions to people under age sixty. Note, though, that being a white or black can *never* be considered a BFOQ for a job.

Race and Color Discrimination

Race discrimination is generally defined as treating someone differently because they have racial origins in Africa or Asia. But protection based on race also extends to American Indians, Eskimos, Native Hawaiians, and even Caucasians. "Color" discrimination implies different treatment based on the relative lightness or darkness of one's skin. Because this second form of discrimination is rare, this discussion will be limited to race.

Most people who attempt to recover damages due to racial discrimination at work will do so through Title VII. Accordingly, the disparate treatment and disparate impact theories discussed earlier are relevant for their cases. However, the **Civil Rights Act of 1866** provides another avenue to sue your employer for race-related discrimination. The advantage of this law is that it often allows victims of race discrimination to collect greater damages.

Racial *harassment* is also prohibited by Title VII. Although being taunted or insulted with a racial slur will not by itself be enough to win your suit, behavior that is severe and pervasive enough to create an abusive work environment might. The standards for proving sexual harassment, presented in chapter 5, are also applicable for cases of racial harassment.

Sex Discrimination

Sex discrimination is a broad term that encompasses different treatment based on sex in all areas of the employment relation—hiring, firing, layoffs, training, pay and benefits, promotion, and discipline—as well as pregnancy discrimination and sexual harassment. Title VII makes all such practices illegal.

Additionally, a special statute covers sex discrimination in pay, called the Equal Pay Act, which is fully discussed in chapter 16.

Like race discrimination claims, most sex discrimination claims are analyzed under the disparate treatment and disparate impact theories. However, sexual harassment is analyzed differently so this book devotes a separate chapter to the subject.

Noteworthy also is the issue of pregnancy discrimination. Employers can save money by not hiring pregnant women and/or by discharging employees who become pregnant. They would argue that pregnant women use more sick days, are tired more often, and are generally less productive than nonpregnant employees. After having a child, new mothers might demand family leave, or they might not return to work at all. And if they do return to work, they'll probably be late a lot, or leaving early, or having day care problems, or will be preoccupied with a host of other things that will reduce their effectiveness.

So the argument goes. For all these reasons, many employers seek to minimize the number of pregnant women and new mothers in their workplaces. That's why we have the **Pregnancy Discrimination Act** (an amendment to Title VII). This law requires employers to treat pregnancy like any other disability. Employers cannot discriminate against their pregnant employees; moreover, special accommodations may be required for pregnant employees. Employers can suffer several financial punishments if found guilty of discriminating against pregnant women.

Religious Discrimination

Title VII protects people from job discrimination based on their religious beliefs. The law not only applies to followers of the more mainstream religions (such as Christianity, Judaism, and Islam), but shields everyone who has a sincere conviction and who seeks to abide by the tenets of his or her religion. Atheists too are afforded protection by Title VII.

Most claims of religious discrimination arise when a job duty conflicts with a religious belief. Some religions prohibit work on a Sabbath and/or holy days, for example, and other religions bar the payment of union dues. The accommodation of these religious beliefs could create scheduling problems for the employer or morale problems with other members of the work force if the religious employee is given special treatment by the employer. Employers are seldom left with satisfactory ways to resolve such conflicts.

The law, however, says that they have a duty to try. Let's take the example of a Seventh Day Adventist who will not work on Saturdays. If his job requires weekend work, the employer and the employee have a problem. But the employer cannot simply fire him. His employer must look for some way to accommodate the employee's request not to work on Saturdays. Moving him to a different shift may be an option; a transfer to another position that doesn't require weekend work would be another option. Employers can be as creative as they would like to meet special religious needs. But they can't discriminate against you or dismiss you for your request for relief from a job and religion conflict, and they can't ignore your situation.

Title VII requires your employer to accommodate you as long as that accommodation imposes no more than a minimal cost on the business. What's a "minimal cost"? There's no clear definition that fits all situations, but the Supreme Court has given us a sense of just how little is demanded of employers. Paying another worker overtime to replace that Seventh Day Adventist on Saturdays is *more than a minimal cost,* and denying a more senior employee a shift preference so that the Seventh Day Adventist could be transferred is also *more than a minimal cost.* In other words, the employer's duty to accommodate your religious beliefs does not extend very far.

National Origin Discrimination

It is not legal to discriminate against a person because of his or her ethnic heritage. That means an employer can't deny you a job (or discriminate against you in other ways) simply because you're Italian, Latino, or Chinese.

Employers can usually require you to be able to speak English because communication between you and your coworkers and between supervisors and their subordinates is often necessary for the safe and efficient operation of a business. For some jobs, employers can also demand that you speak English and only English while performing work that involves contact with customers or clients. But employers would be open to a charge of national origin discrimination if they imposed a "speak only English" rule where there is no business necessity for such a policy.

Discrimination on the basis of citizenship is prohibited by the **Immigration Reform and Control Act** (IRCA). This means that if you're not a U.S. citizen, but you are permitted to work here, employers cannot treat you differently. IRCA does make it unlawful for employers to hire undocumented aliens, though, so discrimination against these people is not only legal, it's mandated.

What to Do about Job Discrimination

If you're one of the unfortunate workers who has suffered discrimination because of your race, color, sex, religion, or national origin, **you do not have to endure it.** You have options. You can confront the perpetrator of the discrimination if you think that will help. Or you can go over this person's head to someone who may be more sympathetic to your concerns. For some of you, though, these internal remedies may simply cause you more grief or may even cost you your job. Others of you may have already lost your job or may have never gotten the job you wanted because of discrimination. There are other avenues to follow in the pursuit of justice.

Government agencies exist to ensure that your rights are protected. Pick up the phone and call both your state human rights commission (listed in Appendix A) and the U.S. Equal Employment Opportunity Commission. Be forewarned, though— you'll probably have to deal with perpetual busy signals, recorded messages, and hip-deep bureaucracy.

You have 180 days from the time you last suffered discriminatory treatment to file your charge with the EEOC. In some cases, this time limit can be extended to 300 days, but do try to stay within the 180-day limit, just to be safe. If you have a state commission that handles such complaints, the EEOC will require you to give the state 60 days to resolve the problem before it will act on your complaint.

When the EEOC acts (and because it is swamped with complaints and understaffed, it may take a while), you can expect that they'll notify your employer of the charge; they'll investigate it by interviewing your witnesses and the employer's witnesses; and, if they find sufficient reason to believe that unlawful discrimination has occurred, they'll attempt to reach an out-of-court settlement between you and your employer. If that doesn't work, the EEOC will either pursue legal action on your behalf (free of charge) or, if you prefer, will issue you a "right-to-sue" notice that says they have found evidence of discriminatory treatment. You can use this notice to pursue a private lawsuit. Suing on your own will cost you money, but it will provide faster relief.

It's important to note that you can still bring a discrimination suit against your employer even without this right-to-sue notice. But you *must* file a charge with the EEOC before taking any private legal action.

Regardless of how you choose to pursue your case, heed this one critical piece of advice: *write down everything that happens at work that might affect your case.* Collect as many relevant memos, performance evaluations, and disciplinary warnings as you can. Save your pink slip and your employee handbook. You'll be asked to recall a lot of information about what happened when, and who overheard what throughout this process. Documentation and tangible evidence of your performance and of company policies will be invaluable to you.

And if you win, you could be awarded up to $300,000 plus legal fees, plus back pay, plus that promotion or job that you didn't get. The size of your award will depend on the size of your employer and what a jury feels is fair. Although going after your employer may sound tempting, remember that you have no guarantee that you will win your case: discrimination is often tough to prove. If you're just looking to get an unfair situation resolved in your favor, in some cases it will make more sense to try to deal directly with your employer. If that's not possible and you choose to take legal action, prepare yourself for a long and perhaps costly battle.

Summary

This chapter has covered the protection available through Title VII and has described how to pursue and to prove your case. But employment discrimination law does not begin and end with Title VII. Almost every state has its own discrimination laws, some which simply mirror Title VII but apply to more employers, others that extend well beyond its boundaries. Hundreds of cities and counties nationwide also have antidiscrimination ordinances on the books. Many of these protections, along with other federal employment discrimination laws, are discussed in the next chapter. However, because this area of the law is so vast, you may find that a question about your specific circumstances has not been fully addressed. To get it answered, call your state human rights commission or the EEOC.

Terminology of Discrimination Law

Title VII   The part of the Civil Rights Act of 1964 that deals with employment issues. It outlaws job discrimination on the basis of race, color, sex, religion, and national origin.

Protected Group   A term that refers to the categories of individuals covered by Title VII and the other antidiscrimination laws. Some examples of "protected groups" are blacks, whites, women, men, Catholics, Jews, Latinos, those over forty, and the disabled.

Disparate Treatment   A type of discrimination in which an employer intentionally treats someone differently because of that person's race, color, sex, religion, national origin, age, or disability.

Disparate Impact   A type of discrimination in which an employer either intentionally or unintentionally harms the employment opportunities of a protected group.

BFOQ   "Bona Fide Occupational Qualification." This is an employer defense to a discrimination suit that basically allows an entire protected group to be excluded from a job because of the dire business consequences that would result from hiring people from this group.

EEOC   The "Equal Employment Opportunity Commission." This is the federal agency that investigates and prosecutes violation of Title VII.

Other Common Questions about Job Discrimination

Q: Affirmative action plans give preferential treatment to some people because of their race or sex. Isn't this exactly what's prohibited by Title VII?

A: The intent of Title VII is to reverse the historic discrimination against women and minorities. It tries to achieve workplace equality for everyone. Even though affirmative action by definition makes the playing field uneven, it is, arguably, consistent with the original intent of Title VII. It attempts to remedy past discrimination and to achieve workplace equality in the long run. Therefore, the U.S. Supreme Court has upheld the legality of affirmative action plans.

These plans are only legal, though, when four conditions are met: (1) when women and/or minorities are initially underrepresented in the employer's workforce; (2) when affirmative action hiring is not done solely by race and sex statistics, but also considers qualifications; (3) when men and nonminorities are not barred from advancement and are not fired to be replaced with women and minorities; and (4) when the plan is adopted as a temporary policy until the employer's workforce achieves a balance.

Q. I was told I didn't get a promotion because of my performance, but I think it was because I'm a woman. How do I know if I have a case?

A. Sometimes employers will refuse to promote you (or will fire you, or will deny you employment) for more than one reason.

The stated reason will usually involve your performance or qualifications, but there may be a discriminatory reason underlying their decision.

Courts call these "mixed-motive" cases because there appears to be both a legitimate and an illegal motive for the employer's action. In these cases, you have to first show that your gender (or race, or whatever) played a part in their decision. If you can do that, your employer must then show that the same decision would have been reached if you were male (or white, or whatever). If it can't do this, you will win the case. If it can do it, it will win; however, your employer may still have to pay your attorney fees if you demonstrated that your sex (or race, or whatever) was a factor in its decisions.

Q: Does Title VII apply to public-sector workers?

State and local government workers whose employers have at least fifteen employees are covered by Title VII. In other words, Title VII covers almost every state and municipal employee. Federal government workers are protected from employment discrimination, but the procedures and remedies differ a bit from those presented in this chapter.

Public employees can also make out discrimination claims through the U.S. and state constitutions, as well as through the Civil Rights Act of 1866. These statutes guarantee that the government will treat all of its employees fairly.

4

Other Kinds
of Discrimination

*Bob walked into his initial managers' meeting full of an-
ticipation and good ideas. To his surprise, though, the first order
of business had nothing to do with getting new defense
contracts.*

*"It's come to my attention that one of the workers in
engineering has cancer," Bob's boss said.*

*"Cancer!" a vice-president responded. "Do you know what
that could do to our insurance rates?!"*

*"I know, I know," replied the boss. "Bob, you're in charge
of engineering now. Take care of this. And be sure the guy gets
two-weeks' severance."*

Fortunately, there's more to employment discrimination law
than what's in Title VII. As indicated in chapter 1, it is illegal
for your employer (or prospective employer) to consider a host
of issues when making employment decisions that affect you.
There are many things about your life that have nothing to do
with how you perform a job. And, quite frankly, most of that
information is just none of your employer's business.

So you drive a foreign car—why should *that* matter? Or
you're divorced, or a Republican, or fifty years old. These things
don't affect your ability to do a job. It gets a little more complicated, though, if you're in a wheelchair, or if you have AIDS, or

if you're a convicted felon. When hiring teachers, for example, should a school board be able to discriminate against those who have convicted of a crime? Can an employer hiring computer programmers discriminate against a blind man? Can a company get rid of someone who is sick with cancer because his or her illness is driving up the company's insurance premiums? Just where does the law draw the line between legitimate and illegitimate considerations?

Title VII's prohibition on race, color, sex, religion, and national origin discrimination left many gaps in employment discrimination law. Other federal statutes and some state statutes have attempted to fill those gaps.

Disability Discrimination

The **Americans with Disabilities Act** (ADA), signed into law by President Bush, is regarded as perhaps the most far-reaching federal employment law enacted since the 1960s. The ADA protects all disabled individuals from job discrimination by any employer who has at least fifteen employees. The law applies to private-sector and state and local government employers, as well as to labor unions and employment agencies. Because this law is so new, the boundaries of what's legal and what's not legal are still a bit blurry. Therefore, it's important to recognize that this section offers you only general guidance about how the courts and the Equal Employment Opportunity Commission (EEOC) will *probably* evaluate you disability case. But even with that caveat, one thing is certain: disability discrimination is now illegal and those who are found guilty of such discrimination can face penalties of up to $300,000.

There are two key questions in this area: Are you "disabled"? and if so, What does your employer have to do to accommodate you disability? The answer to the first question is spelled out in the ADA. A disabled person is one who:

1. has a physical or mental impairment that substantially limits one or more major life activities, or
2. has a record of such an impairment, or

3. is regarded by the employer or potential employer as having such an impairment.

Because this terminology is so vague, the EEOC has attempted to explain what the individual terms mean:

"Physical Impairment"   Physiological conditions or disorders like problems with speech, sight, hearing, and walking, and diseases like epilepsy, cerebral palsy, multiple sclerosis, diabetes, cancer, heart conditions, obesity, tuberculosis, and HIV/AIDS. Physical problems that are neither permanent nor chronic (like broken bones, sprains, or the flu) will not qualify.

"Mental Impairment"   Mental or psychological disorders like retardation, dyslexia, learning disabilities, and alcoholism. Drug abuse, homosexuality, bisexuality, transvestitism, transsexuality, pedophilia, exhibitionism, voyeurism, gender identity disorders, sexual behavior disorders, pyromania, kleptomania, and compulsive gambling *are not* considered impairments of any kind under the ADA.

"Substantially Limits"   Either the individual must not be able to perform a major life activity (like walking) that those in the general population can perform, or the ability of the individual to perform that activity must be severely limited.

"Major Life Activity"   Included are caring for yourself, walking, speaking, seeing, hearing, being able to perform manual tasks, breathing, learning, and having the ability to work.

"Record of Such an Impairment"   Having a history of a physical or mental impairment (as in the case of a former cancer patient).

"Regarded as Having an Impairment"   Where the employer believes that you are impaired, whether you are or not (for instance, if the employer was responding to a rumor that you had cancer).

Returning to the case of the employee at Bob's firm, then, to be protected by the ADA he must have a physical or mental impairment, or have a record of the impairment, or be regarded as having the impairment. We're told that the employee has cancer, which counts as a physical impairment. And if he doesn't, he's still regarded as having the impairment by the employer. So he meets that criterion.

But to be considered "disabled," his impairment must also substantially limit a major life activity. In the long run, cancer and other chronic diseases will limit life activities. In all likelihood, most courts should accept the contention that people with these diseases pass the "substantially limited" test because it is the intent of the ADA to protect these individuals. It is conceivable, though, that a particular judge or jury would find that if the disease isn't affecting the individual now, that individual is not covered by the ADA.

Assuming that this employee is "disabled," and therefore covered by the ADA, he's going to win his discrimination suit unless his employer can demonstrate a legitimate, nondiscriminatory reason for his termination (as in all "disparate treatment" cases; see chapter 3). The EEOC has said that a company's increased insurance costs *will not* qualify as a legitimate reason. However, things like poor performance, insubordination, excessive absenteeism, or theft are appropriate grounds for discharge.

Which brings us to the second big question: if you are disabled, what does your employer (or prospective employer) have to do to accommodate your needs? The ADA imposes a duty on employers to seek out and to pay for a *reasonable accommodation* that allows you to do your job. That means the employer must determine what job functions are limited because of your disability, consult with you to identify possible accommodations, and consider your preference concerning accommodations. A reasonable accommodation could mean purchasing special equipment, reassigning you to another job, restructuring you current job, or even hiring a personal assistant for you. *You will be considered "qualified" for a job if you can perform the essential functions of the job with this accommodation in place.*

But there are limits to an employer's duty. As you might expect, some accommodations don't come cheaply. Therefore, the employer must accommodate you only if the accommodation doesn't pose significant difficulty or require excessive expense. To make that determination, a court will take into consideration the cost of the accommodation, the employer's financial resources, the nature of the employer's operation, and the effect of the accommodation on other employees.

So there's a lot to the issue of disability discrimination. But because we're dealing with uncharted territory here, you'll want to check with the EEOC to get the most up-to-date advice about any case you might have. Also, because many states have disability discrimination laws that may offer you even greater protection than the ADA offers, it's a good idea to discuss your case · with your state human rights commission as well. Charitable and support groups targeted to specific disabled populations, such as those for the deaf, the blind, and people suffering from cancer, may also be valuable resources for obtaining free advice.

Age Discrimination

Shortly after the passage of Title VII, Congress enacted the **Age Discrimination in Employment Act** (ADEA) which made it unlawful for any employer that had at least twenty employees to discriminate against those between the ages of forty and sixty-five. Later, the law was broadened to protect anyone who was forty or older. So if MTV decided that it didn't want to hire anyone over age thirty-nine to be a video-jockey, that's age discrimination. But it's also age discrimination to set a mandatory retirement age or to put any special restrictions on older workers. This applies to hiring, training, pay and benefits, promotion, discipline, and discharge. Age discrimination cases are evaluated using the same standards of proof developed for Title VII (disparate treatment, disparate impact, and BFOQ; see chapter 3). An example of a disparate treatment would be refusing to hire someone because the person is fifty-five years old. Disparate impact cases are a little more common and typically arise when an employer lays off workers and a disproportionate number of them are over forty, or when it scales back its pension plan or other benefits that have their greatest relevance to older workers.

Occasionally, an employer will implement a policy that says no one over, say, sixty will be hired for this job. Normally, this would be a case of blatant age discrimination. But employers of pilots, flight engineers, and bus drivers have actually been able to justify such a policy in court by using the BFOQ defense, as explained in chapter 3.

In addition to the ADEA, a majority of states have passed their own laws against age discrimination. For younger workers who are feeling a bit slighted by the ADEA, there's also some good news: twenty states and the District of Columbia protect workers under forty as well as those over forty: the states are Alaska, Connecticut, Florida, Hawaii, Iowa, Kansas, Maine, Maryland, Michigan, Minnesota, Montana, Nebraska, New Hampshire, New Jersey, New Mexico, New York, North Carolina, Oregon, Vermont, and Virginia. State human rights commissions are responsible for administering these laws.

State Laws against Discrimination

Every state except Alabama, Arkansas, Georgia, and Mississippi has laws prohibiting job discrimination. Many of these laws simply mirror the protections set forth in Title VII but apply to smaller employers (recall that Title VII only applies to employers with fifteen or more employees). Some states, as noted above, regulate disability and age discrimination too. Table 4.1 illustrates which states offer additional protections.

Marital status discrimination is defined in most states as treating someone differently because he or she is married, single, divorced, separated or widowed. Usually, such a law will prevent an employer from paying married workers more than unmarried workers doing the same job, or from offering better benefits to married workers. Employers in these states also cannot adopt policies that have a disparate impact on people by marital status (hiring only individuals without children, for example, could severely harm the employment opportunities of married people).

Smokers have legal protections in twenty-one states. Although almost all states either permit or require employers to ban smoking in the workplace, many states protect people who smoke off-duty from job discrimination. Employers in these states can't refuse to hire you because you smoke. In fact, they

TABLE 4.1
State Laws Against Discrimination

State	Marital Status	Smoking	Sexual Orientation
Alaska	X		
Arizona	X*		
California	X		X
Colorado		X	
Connecticut	X	X	X
Delaware	X		
Dist. of Columbia	X		X
Florida	X		
Hawaii	X		X
Illinois	X	X	
Indiana		X	
Kansas	X		
Kentucky		X	
Louisiana		X	
Maine		X	
Maryland	X		
Massachusetts	X		X
Michigan	X		
Minnesota	X		X
Mississippi		X	
Montana	X		
Nebraska	X		
Nevada		X	
New Hampshire	X	X	
New Jersey	X	X	X
New Mexico	X	X	
New York	X		
Oklahoma		X	
Oregon	X	X	X**
Rhode Island		X	
South Carolina		X	
South Dakota		X	
Tennessee		X	
Vermont			X
Virginia	X	X	
Washington	X		
Wisconsin	X		X

*The Arizona law applies to state employees only.
**Oregon has a law that outlaws discrimination based on whom you associate with outside of work. This law covers discrimination based on the sexual orientation of an employee.

shouldn't even ask the question in an interview. With regard to benefits, employers can't deny smokers life or health insurance if everyone else gets it. However, because workers who smoke raise the employer's insurance premiums, an employer could legally require smokers to pay more for their benefit package.

Employment discrimination on the basis of sexual orientation is outlawed in only a handful of states. Several cities and counties across the nation also prohibit it, with some specifically designating that "domestic partners" of gay and lesbian employees are entitled to the same benefits as dependents of heterosexual employees. This is a new and developing area of employee protection, so it is likely that more states will adopt such laws in the future.

Finally, there are a number of miscellaneous protections available to you depending on where you live. The states that address discrimination on the basis of arrest and conviction record, welfare status, political affiliation, family obligations, and other individual characteristics are listed in table 1.2 on page 6.

Summary

If you're the victim of some type of discrimination that doesn't fall neatly into one of the categories specified by Title VII, there may still be hope for your case. As detailed in this chapter, several other discrimination statutes exist to combat arbitrary treatment by employers. If any of the laws discussed here applies to your situation, call the appropriate federal or state agency for assistance. And if none apply, check out chapter 7. Sometimes "common law" protects you when statutes don't.

5

Sexual Harassment

"I'm pretty busy right now," he said to her." "Can you get me a cup of coffee?"

"I'm not your secretary!" she replied, clearly irritated by the request.

"Well then," he responded with a smirk, "I guess a look at those 38D's is out of the question."

Some of you are grinning right now. Others of you aren't. And it's a safe bet that the two groups are not split strictly along gender lines.

That's the nature of this complex issue. People view the interaction between men and women differently. Some would dismiss the man's statement as a harmless joke, while others, especially those who have had to endure such behavior, would see it as humiliating and degrading. The problem to be faced when attempting to define sexual harassment is that everyone has his or her own opinion of what is acceptable conduct in and out of the workplace. How do we draw a single line that applies to everyone? It's been tough, but the courts have drawn that line.

The Two Types of Sexual Harassment

Sexual harassment is considered to be a form of sex discrimination. Accordingly, as noted in chapter 3, it is illegal under Title VII. There are two general types of sexual harassment:

"quid pro quo" harassment and "abusive work environment harassment."

"Quid pro quo" literally means "this for that." It works as follows: a supervisor or a manager promises a subordinate a promotion or a raise in return for sexual favors, "this" promotion for "that" favor. It also covers threats made by supervisors and managers: you get to keep "this" job for "that" favor (or, you'll be hired for "this" job in exchange for "that" favor).

Unfortunately, this kind of slimy behavior is a reality in many workplaces. Bosses sometimes abuse their power by seeking to exchange specific job benefits for sexual relations. But quid pro quo harassment is illegal and your employer is liable for fines and damages of up to $300,000.

The second type of sexual harassment, the creation of an abusive or hostile work environment, does not involve the granting of a job benefit and is not limited to the actions or words of supervisors and managers. The opening scenario exemplifies how someone begins to create an abusive work environment. An employee—it could be your boss, a coworker at your own level, or even a subordinate—through unwelcome verbal or physical conduct of a sexual nature, makes your life at work uncomfortable. When such conduct rises to a level that a court would consider "abusive" or "hostile," it becomes illegal sexual harassment. No specific promises or threats need be made—this type of harassment simply involves the alteration of your overall work environment.

How to Prove Sexual Harassment

Proving quid pro quo harassment requires you to show that:

1. you were subject to harassment because of your sex, and
2. the harassment involved a specific condition of your employment (either one that was promised or one that was threatened), and
3. a supervisor or manager was responsible for the harassment, and
4. there was a definite connection between the harassment and the specific employment condition.

The first three parts are self-explanatory. You have to establish that this exchange actually happened. The fourth may be a little trickier.

Let's say you were denied a raise. You claim that the raise was denied because you refused your boss's sexual advances. To win a sexual harassment case, you must prove that your refusal led to the boss's decision to deny you a raise.

Or let's say you're in a job interview and the interviewer propositions you. You flatly reject this sexual advance and later learn that you didn't get the job. To prove sexual harassment, you have to show that one event caused the other. In essence, your task is to show that you would have gotten the job if the harassment had never occurred.

Similarly, winning an abusive work environment case also requires you to demonstrate that the harassment did take place and that a specific individual (or set of individuals) was responsible for it. After that, rather than focusing on one aspect of your job that was affected (as in quid pro quo), the court or the jury will evaluate the impact on your entire work environment to determine if it has become "abusive." To do this, *all the circumstances surrounding the harassment must be considered* to answer three questions:

1. **How *pervasive* was the conduct?** Did it happen only once or twice? Did it happen daily? Just how frequently were you harassed?
2. **How *severe* was the conduct?** Did he simply ask you out on a date or was there more to it? Was the harassment verbal, physical, or both? If it was only verbal, what did he say and how did he say it? If it was physical, where did he touch you?
3. **Was the conduct *unwelcome*?** Did you invite his advances? Were you receptive to his suggestions? How did you dress and speak? Did you voluntarily discuss sexual topics? Had the two of you had sexual relations before?

It's important to note here that *no one* of these questions by itself will determine the outcome of the case. A woman who regularly dresses in a seductive manner can still be the victim of sexual harassment. Infrequent behavior may still be illegal behavior, but a single pat on the bottom is probably not enough by itself to establish sexual harassment.

What the court looks for is unwelcomeness and a combination of pervasiveness and severity. The more pervasive the conduct, the less severe it has to be to prove your case. The more severe the conduct, the less pervasive it must be to prove your case.

Returning to the opening scenario should help to clarify this point. Because we don't have more facts, we'll assume that the comment meets the "unwelcomeness" standard (a pretty safe assumption). If that's the case, we turn to the issues of pervasiveness and severity. If this comment was an isolated incident that hadn't happened before and never happened again, the woman would stand little chance of winning a sexual harassment case in court. The man's conduct might be considered reasonably severe, but it was not pervasive. On the other hand, if this man continued to make lewd remarks, or if he started leaving obscene notes for his coworker, or if he began following her home from work, she'd have a stronger case. A court will look either for pervasive patterns of behavior or for isolated conduct that is so offensive that they or it create(s) an "abusive" work environment.

Complications arise when what one person could tolerate might cause another person to completely fall apart. Here, again, we come up against the problem of setting one standard that applies to everyone. The law resolves this problem with an objective standard called a **"reasonable person test"** (or, in some places, a "reasonable woman test"). In court, it doesn't matter if the alleged victim considers the working environment abusive. What does matter is if the "reasonable person" would find that the conduct in question created an "abusive" work environment. If so, the conduct is probably illegal.

This standard allows courts to throw out cases of people who may be hypersensitive to well-intentioned compliments like "You look very nice today." It also means that making jokes in bad taste or asking a coworker for a date are usually not unlawful. Most courts will not find that these things create an abusive environment for the "reasonable person."

In summary: to prove an abusive work environment case you must demonstrate unwelcome behavior of a sexual nature that is so pervasive and severe that a reasonable person would find the work environment to be abusive. If you are frustrated that these are pretty ambiguous guidelines, you're in good company. A U.S. Supreme Court justice recently wrote, "Abusive . . . does not seem to me a very clear standard." For now, however, that's all we have.

Employer Liability

So even if you can prove your case, what do you get? As mentioned earlier, if the harassment is of the quid pro quo variety, your employer is liable—period. In addition to attorney fees and court costs, the maximum you can receive depends on the size of your employer: 15–100 employees, $50,000; 101–200 employees, $100,000; 201–500 employees, $200,000; and more than 500 employees, $300,000.

The same maximums apply if you prove sexual harassment under the abusive work environment theory. However, unlike quid pro quo, you cannot automatically collect from your employer. Although the rules are still a little vague, it appears that an employer will be liable for the abusive environment created by a middle or a high-level supervisor or manager. The employer will also be liable for the actions of a low-level supervisor if the employer knew or should have known that the harassment was taking place. Thus to protect yourself, you should alert somebody in authority in the human resources department if you are being harassed.

Additionally, the employer has a duty to discourage sexual harassment and to respond to complaints with prompt, effective action. Therefore, your employer should have a strong sexual harassment policy in place that includes some way for you to complain to management about harassment. Once an employer learns of harassment, the employer must investigate the situation and do whatever is necessary to eliminate the harassment. The employer doesn't have to fire the alleged harasser; a warning, a transfer, or disciplinary action can be an appropriate response. The bottom line is that further misconduct must be prevented. If an employer has no harassment policy, or if it does not properly respond to complaints of harassment, it will be held liable if the harasser is not a supervisor.

Summary

The word is out: sexual harassment is illegal and employers who don't do a good enough job preventing it will face costly lawsuits. As a result, greater sensitivity about this issue and some internal procedures for dealing with it have evolved.

If someone is harassing you, don't be afraid to speak up and to use whatever grievance procedure your employer has in place. If there isn't one, create your own: Complain to the highest person you have access to and tell him or her the whole story. Just to be safe, file your complaint to him or her in writing too. Once the employer has been put on notice, it must get results. And if it doesn't, call the U.S. Equal Employment Opportunity Commission. They will.

Other Common Questions about Sexual Harassment

Q: Do these sexual harassment rules apply only to women?

A: Definitely not. Although it's rare, there have been cases of women sexually harassing men at work. Male victims are entitled to the same protections as female victims.

A related question involves same-sex sexual harassment, which, according to most courts that have heard these cases, is also illegal. Courts will evaluate claims of men who are harassed by men and women who are harassed by women in the same way that they evaluate more traditional sexual harassment claims.

Q: Does sexual harassment have to take place at work for it to be illegal?

A: Whether your boss or a coworker harasses you at work, in the parking lot, or in the supermarket doesn't matter. The real questions are the harassment's impact on your work environment and if there was any quid pro quo involved.

Since Title VII only applies to work-related situations, though, you cannot rely on it to protect you if you're harassed by someone who has nothing to do with your workplace. That means if a neighbor is looking in your bedroom window at night, you can't win a sexual harassment suit like the ones discussed in this chapter. However, there are other legal remedies for this type of behavior.

Q: I heard that in order to prove sexual harassment you have to show that your work performance was impaired and that you suffered psychological damage. Is this true?

A: Neither is true anymore. The U.S. Supreme Court has put to rest both of these myths. Although impaired work performance or psychological damage is relevant evidence, you no longer have to prove either of these things to show that your work environment was abusive.

Q: Do I have to tolerate pin-up calendars and posters of naked women at work?

A: The courts have been saying that these types of things create an abusive work environment. Because it's your employer's duty to keep your workplace free from anything that might produce an abusive or hostile atmosphere, your employer might be liable for this form of sexual harassment.

In short, evidence of sexual harassment isn't limited to physical and/or verbal behavior. Posters, obscene T-shirts, messages on your locker, and even drawings or writing on a wall are all relevant in determining if a work environment is abusive.

Q: At work, I see guys casually looking down women's sweaters and at women's rear ends all the time. It makes me uncomfortable. Is this sexual harassment?

A: Somewhere between "uncomfortable" and "abusive" is a dividing line that separates the lawful from the unlawful. A lustful glance or a rude joke may make you uncomfortable, but it will win you no money in court because the law does not require employers to regulate every inconsiderate action. Therefore, in all likelihood, no judge, jury, or agency is going to find this conduct by itself to be illegal.

6

Employee Appearance

His hair is too long. All the women in this office should wear makeup. Our sales reps must wear business suits if we're to be taken seriously. A no-beard policy will make our waiters look cleaner, and high heels should improve the legs of our waitresses. Wow, that stewardess is fat! Our company needs to do something about it.

Employer grooming and appearance codes exist for all sorts of reasons. Some reasons seem valid, some seem arbitrary, and others seem downright repugnant. The stated purpose for such rules generally involves concerns for public image, customer satisfaction, or safety. A law firm, for example, may worry about client perceptions of the professionalism of lawyers who wear blue jeans. A restaurant owner may fear that customers will associate the cook's long, unkempt hair with unappetizing food and never return to his restaurant. A fire captain may fear that a fireman's respirator mask may not work properly if he has a full beard. The reasons for establishing appearance standards are as varied as the employers we work for. Such standards, though, are a frequent source of trouble for many employers.

When do appearance rules violate the law? **The short answer is: appearance codes violate the law when they pose a greater hardship to one group of people than to another group and have no real business justification.** A policy regulating flight cabin attendants' weight, for instance, must apply equally to men and women. If it does, it's probably legal; if it does not, it's probably sex discrimination.

Employee appearance codes that have not held up in court were most often invalidated because they burdened a particular gender, religious, or racial group. Employer rules concerning hair, height and weight, and attire—the most commonly regulated aspects of employee appearance—are discussed below.

Hair and Facial Hair

Have you ever seen a Domino's pizza delivery boy with a beard? If so, you probably could have gotten a few free pizzas by reporting the sighting to Domino's corporate management. Until recently, Domino's maintained a no-beard policy. But when this policy was challenged in court on racial grounds, it was ruled discriminatory.

Racial grounds? Don't men of all races wear beards? How could a no-beard policy pose a greater burden to any one race? That was my first response to the court's ruling. Then I was introduced to the term pseudofolliculitis barbae (PFB). PFB is a skin condition that makes it painful to shave. Therefore, men with PFB often grow beards. Because PFB affects many more blacks than whites, Domino's no-beard policy could disproportionately screen out blacks from employment.

The ruling in the Domino's case does not mean that all no-beard policies are illegal. Some companies have been able to convince courts that business conditions necessitate a clean appearance, and the courts have bought into this argument notwithstanding evidence of PFB.

Others, especially Jewish and Sikh males, have challenged facial hair prohibitions by claiming that their religious beliefs require them to wear a beard. Consistent with the religious discrimination analysis described in chapter 3, courts have asked the employers in question whether accommodating the employee's beliefs would constitute an undue hardship to the business. Generally, the more legitimate the justification for the policy, the less likely the employee will win.

Hair length is another dicey issue. Again, provided that the employer applies the rules evenhandedly, the policy will usually stand up in court. Does this mean that if a business prohibits long hair for men it must also do so for women? Not exactly. Judges do recognize that men and women are different. Absolute standards do not need to apply across genders for a policy to be deemed fair. Rather, a business can insist that its employees' hair styles conform to "societal standards" without the policy adversely affecting anyone. In other words, it can require *short,* neatly kept hair for men, while allowing *any-length,* neatly kept hair for women.

Height and Weight Restrictions

As noted above, weight regulations, if they are to be considered valid, must apply to both sexes. They must also factor in the differences in height-to-weight ratios for men and women, and they must be founded on some legitimate business reason. Because the last of these conditions is often a difficult burden for the employer to meet, such policies are rare. A similar analysis applies to height restrictions.

Noteworthy, too, is the possible impact of the Americans with Disabilities Act (ADA) on employee weight cases. You'll recall from chapter 4 that the courts have just begun to determine what qualifies as a disability under the ADA. It is entirely plausible that an over- or underweight person could successfully claim to be disabled and make the case that a company weight policy is a form of disability discrimination.

Dress Codes

Rules that apply to everyone, that are consistent with societal norms, and that are justified by business concerns are typically considered legitimate. Businesses are afforded a lot of leeway in determining the boundaries of acceptable attire, so long as they do not specifically burden any employee group. Can they force men to wear a tie? Yes. Women to wear a dress? Usually. Either or both sexes to wear a business suit? Yes. Women to wear pantyhose? Probably. A uniform? As long as it applies to both sexes.

How about compelling women to wear provocative outfits? The knee-jerk response from most of us "Absolutely not!" The legal response, though, is, "It depends." Do men have to wear uniforms as well? Is there a business-related reason for the policy? Does any harm come to those wearing the outfit specifically because of their attire? A court will carefully weigh all the relevant circumstances surrounding an employee appearance policy before rendering its judgment.

Presumably, in this case, female accountants, lawyers, or assembly line workers could successfully challenge the notion that plunging necklines enhance profits. Cocktail waitresses, on the other hand, possibly could not (but it has happened in New Jersey). Unless the outfit led to customer harassment, the bar owner's marketing strategy might remain in force.

Summary

So your boss is compelling you to wear high heels instead of flats, or a white shirt rather than a colored one. Examine the stated reason for the rules, but more importantly, look for *balance* in the policy. The bottom line is this: the law favors your employer on this issue, even if the policy seems absurd or pointless. Unless you can make a clear case that the appearance code places an additional hardship on a protected group of individuals (women, blacks, Jews, or whatever), chances are it's not a winnable fight. Remember: the law doesn't always require employer policies to be logical; it only requires them to be consistent.

Other Common Questions about Employee Appearance Rules

Q: Can a company tell male employees that they can't wear earrings?

A: The answer may be different ten years from now as societal standards gradually liberalize, but right now the answer is probably yes. Employees who have no contact with the public or with suppliers, though, would stand a better chance of successfully challenging this rule since the employer seemingly would have little business justification for it.

Q: Is it legal to prohibit religious pins, necklaces, and other religious jewelry in the workplace?

A: That's a tough call. Private-sector employees can look to Title VII for protection. A court will weigh the business necessity for this policy against any business hardship that would result from accommodating the employee's desire to continue wearing the jewelry. That is, it will first examine the employer's reason and, if it's found to be a legitimate one, it will then consider the burden of accommodating the employee. If the accommodation imposes more than a minimal cost on the business, the employer's policy will hold up in court (you can refer back to the religious discrimination section of chapter 3 for more detail on this balancing test).

Public-sector employers would have a tougher time enforcing such a rule because public employees, unlike their private-sector counterparts, have constitutional protections at work, one of which is the right to freely express their religious beliefs. Teachers, however, are an exception. Courts have interpreted their religious expression in the public school (through clothing, jewelry, and otherwise) as "establishing religion" in violation of the First Amendment.

7

Wrongful Discharge

To say that Chris was sloshed would be an understatement. But basically, he was a slobbering mess. Still, he managed to sit upright on his barstool and demand another drink. Jim, the bartender, politely told him he'd had too much already and offered to call him a cab.

As a regular customer, Chris was both insulted and outraged. He caused such a scene that the manager had to come over to calm him down. Upon learning that Jim had refused service to a customer, the manager promptly fired him.

As the previous few chapters demonstrated, federal and state governments have written many laws to protect you from unfair treatment. But employers can come up with unfair reasons to fire you faster than politicians can legislate against them. That's why judges have had to step in to fill some of the gaps.

Chapter 2 discussed the concept of "common law," judges' rulings that have the same effect as a statute within a particular court jurisdiction. This chapter will explain what common law protections you have on the job. To better understand them, though, it's important that you read chapter 2 before you read this one.

When Firing an Employee Violates a Public Policy

A man in Oregon was fired for taking time off to serve on a jury. A pharmacist in New Jersey was fired because he refused to leave the drug counter unsupervised. A Texas woman was terminated because she volunteered at an AIDS clinic during her free time. All of these cases have one thing in common: the terminated employee sued for **"wrongful discharge in violation of a public policy."**

That's a mouthful, but when you break it down, the concept isn't very complicated. "Wrongful discharge" means that your employer, according to the law, did something wrong by firing you.

"Public policies" are the principles, values, and goals that underlie our laws. They can be found in statutes, government regulations, court decisions, and our federal and state constitutions. For instance, one of our public policies is to discourage illegal drug use. We advance that policy by making drug use and drug dealing illegal, and by imposing stiff penalties on offenders. Another public policy is to provide a quality education for all children. We've developed a free public education system to attempt to meet this goal. The government has taken a stand on the poor, on free trade, on the environment, and on hundreds of other issues. Those stands are known as "public policy."

So, putting these two concepts together, **"wrongful discharge in violation of public policy" means that the termination would somehow have the effect of undermining one of our country's principles or goals.**

Returning to our fired employees, discharging the man from Oregon violated public policy because it is an important national goal to promptly seat juries. With regard to the pharmacist, his firing violated public policy because there is a New Jersey law that says drug counters must be supervised at all times. An employee can seldom be fired for refusing to do something that's illegal.

But what about that woman from Texas? To win her case, she'd need to show that some public policy exists that encourages assistance to AIDS patients or charity work in general.

Arguably, there might be, but the court in this case didn't buy the argument and, as a result, she lost her case.

Had she worked in another state, she might have won, though. That's the confusing thing about this part of the law. Some states outlaw terminations that violate public policy, but others do not. And to complicate matters even more, *what is considered public policy in one state isn't necessarily considered public policy in another* (for example, New York arguably has a policy encouraging assistance to AIDS patients whereas Texas does not). Table 7.1 lists the states where a termination that violates public policy is illegal.

TABLE 7.1

Protection from Wrongful Discharge

	Public Policy	Employee Handbook	Implied Covenant
Alabama		X	
Alaska	X	X	X
Arizona	X	X	
Arkansas	X		
California	X	X	X
Colorado	X	X	
Connecticut	X	X	X
Delaware	X		
Dist. of Columbia	X	X	
Florida	X		
Georgia			
Hawaii	X		
Idaho	X	X	X
Illinois	X	X	X
Indiana	X		
Iowa	X	X	X
Kansas	X	X	
Kentucky	X	X	
Louisiana			
Maine		X	

TABLE 7.1   *(Continued)*
Protection from Wrongful Discharge

	Public Policy	Employee Handbook	Implied Covenant
Maryland	X	X	
Massachusetts	X	X	X
Michigan	X	X	
Minnesota	X	X	X
Mississippi	X	X	
Missouri	X	X	
Montana	X	X	X
Nebraska	X	X	
Nevada	X	X	X
New Hampshire	X		X
New Jersey	X	X	
New Mexico	X	X	
New York		X	X
North Carolina	X	X	
North Dakota	X	X	
Ohio	X	X	
Oklahoma	X	X	X
Oregon	X	X	
Pennsylvania	X	X	
Rhode Island	X		
South Carolina	X	X	
South Dakota	X	X	
Tennessee	X		
Texas	X		
Utah		X	
Vermont		X	
Virginia	X	X	
Washington	X	X	
West Virginia	X	X	
Wisconsin	X	X	
Wyoming	X	X	

A related concept, although not a common law, is a **"whistle-blower statute."** Let's say that one day you learn that all the radioactive waste you thought your employer was shipping to Indiana for safe disposal is really being dumped into a nearby river. Can you call the police or the state's department of environmental protection? And if you do, can you be fired for such action?

Or consider, for example, the case of a junior accountant who stumbled across the fact that the company president had embezzled most of the firm's pension fund. Can he save the fund and his job at the same time?

Whistleblower laws exist to protect the jobs of employees who report their employer's illegal activities. Several states (they are listed in table 7.2) have passed laws that seek to reduce employer crimes. Typically, though, the law does not permit you to simply run to the government with your story. **You must first approach your boss or supervisor with the problem and request (usually in writing) that the illegal activity cease.** This is, of course, risky for you, but if you skip this step, your job probably

TABLE 7.2
States with Whistleblower Statutes

Arizona*	Kentucky*	North Dakota*
California	Louisiana***	Ohio
Colorado**	Maine	Oregon*
Connecticut	Maryland*	Pennsylvania*
Delaware	Michigan	Rhode Island*
Florida*	Minnesota	South Carolina*
Hawaii	Missouri**	Texas*
Illinois*	Nebraska	Washington**
Indiana	New Hampshire	West Virginia*
Iowa*	New Jersey	Wisconsin**
Kansas**	New York	

*Applies to public employees only.
**Applies to state government employees only.
***Applies only in cases where the employer is breaking an environmental protection law.

won't be protected by the law. You have to give your employer an opportunity to correct the situation before you go elsewhere.

Nor will your job be protected if you go to the press with the story. Although this might appear to be your shot at fame and fortune, the way the laws are written, such action could be your ticket to joblessness. Whistleblower laws protect you only when you go to the appropriate government agency.

If you're right about the action being illegal, and you've gone through the proper channels, you've performed a great service for society. But what if you're wrong? What if you thought radioactive waste was being dumped into the river but it was really only fish food? Often, the initial discussion with your employer will clear this up. However, *if* you still believe that your employer is up to no good, *and* your employer refuses to do anything about it, *then* you can go to the authorities. And yes, your job is still protected even if you are wrong in your suspicions. Your employer can't discriminate against or discharge you for your actions. **In a nutshell, in most states, as long as you *reasonably believe* that you are correct about your employer's illegal activities, and your employer doesn't respond to your complaints, you can't lose your job for blowing the whistle on your employer.**

To sum up this public policy section, then, depending on where you live, you can't be fired for:

- Carrying out a public obligation (like jury duty)
- Refusing to commit an illegal act (like leaving a drug counter unattended)
- Exercising some right or privilege that's in a statute (like filing a workers' compensation claim)
- Reporting a violation of the law by your employer (like illegal dumping).

Your Employee Handbook May Be a Contract

Common law in some states specifically deals with the contents of your employee handbook. You know the one I'm talking about: it's buried in the bottom drawer of your desk. This would be a good time to dig it out because it might be more important than you think.

Courts in several states have said that what an employer declares in its handbook is, in essence, promises to employees. Accordingly, your employer is bound to live up to declarations made in a handbook, just like it is to any contract. What's particularly of interest is any wording in the handbook that talks about steps your employer will take before discharging an employee or that notes that you'll only be fired for a good reason (it might use the term "just cause," which means the same thing). If that's the case, your employer has given up its "employment-at-will" privileges (see chapter 2). You can't be terminated except for just cause.

Bear in mind, though, that only the states listed in table 7.1 consider employee handbooks to be contracts. Also, there's one more consideration to keep in mind: employers can put a disclaimer in their handbook stating that the employer isn't bound to the contents of the handbook. In most states, if the disclaimer is written in plain, understandable English (as compared to legal jargon), and if it makes perfectly clear that the employer doesn't consider the handbook a contract, then in the eyes of the court it probably isn't a contract. In other words, you usually can't hold your employer to what's written in the handbook if it includes a disclaimer. Currently, though, states vary in how explicit the employer's disclaimer must be.

Some States Require All Employers to Treat Employees Fairly

For the moment, forget public policy and forget employee handbooks. Wouldn't it make more sense to just say employers have a duty to be fair with all their employees: to keep promises to employees, to treat all employees alike, and only to fire them for a good reason? That would conceivably cover both public policy and employee handbook issues. Well, a handful of states have done just that. In addition to recognizing these other common law protections discussed above, some state courts have said that there is an **"implied covenant of good faith and fair dealing"** between employers and employees.

That's a pretty formidable term, but it essentially boils down to the employer's duty to treat all employees fairly and consistently. Here are a few examples of how the implied covenant was applied:

> A woman was fired for dating someone at a competitor's firm. However, the woman's company had previously issued a memo that said it would only be concerned with an employee's off-the-job behavior when that behavior affected the employee's work performance. Her performance wasn't affected by the relationship.
>
> Although this memo wasn't part of the employee handbook, the jury found that it was still a promise. It ruled that the "implied covenant" recognized in that state (California) was violated because the employer broke its promise. Because it didn't treat her fairly by the jury's standards, the company had to pay the woman $300,000.
>
> A manager at a food store was put on probation for not properly controlling the store's inventory. He complained that the managers at other stores weren't disciplined when they had similar inventory shortages, and eventually this conflict led to his termination.
>
> The store argued in court that it didn't have to follow anything in the employee handbook because there was a disclaimer there. But the court ruled that the handbook was irrelevant because employers in that state (Montana) had an implied duty to treat employees consistently. Because his firing amounted to imconsistent treatment, and because the employer didn't have a "fair and honest reason for the termination," the manager was awarded $270,000 in damages.

The implied covenant of good faith and fair dealing scares the heck out of employers and, as you can see from the awards in these cases, they have good reason to be scared. Employees can

be awarded a great deal of money when juries, usually domi-
nated by people who are themselves employees, sympathize with
them. However, only a handful of states (those listed in table
7.1) currently impose the implied covenant of good faith on
employers.

Other Employer Violations of Your Rights

In addition to violations of public policy, the employee handbook, and the implied covenant, employers have been successfully sued by their employees on several other grounds.
Although this list appears to cover most employee issues, keep
in mind that these charges are difficult to prove.

Invasion of Privacy occurs when the employer intrudes on the
private affairs of an employee in a way that most people would
find "highly offensive" (see chapter 9).

Defamation occurs when an employer makes false statements
about an employee that result in harm to the employee's reputation (see chapter 12).

Negligent Hiring occurs when an employer hires someone who
the employer knows or should have known was dangerous, dishonest, incompetent, or irresponsible, and then that person
harms a coworker or a customer.

Negligence in Conducting a Performance Appraisal occurs when
the employer during the previous performance evaluation
neglected to inform the employee that he or she would be discharged if his or her performance didn't improve, and then the
employee is later terminated for poor performance.

Intentional Infliction of Emotional Distress (IIED) occurs
when an employer deliberately engages in such outrageous conduct toward an employee that it causes severe emotional
distress.

Negligent Infliction of Emotional Distress (NIED) is similar to
IIED except that the employer doesn't have to deliberately harm
the employee. The emotional distress can result from a reckless
or irresponsible employer action.

- **Fraud** occurs when an employer blatantly misrepresents the conditions of a new job to an applicant to induce the applicant to accept an offer of employment.

- **Malicious Prosecution** occurs when an employer recklessly disregards an employee's rights by falsely accusing an employee of something.

Assault and Battery occurs when an employer intentionally and unlawfully threatens, touches, or strikes an employee without justification and with the intent to injure that employee; assault and battery is often alleged in sexual harassment cases.

False Imprisonment occurs when a supervisor or manager restrains the movement of an employee such that the employee would reasonably fear for his or her safety, property, or reputation.

And If You Win . . .

The woman in California won $300,000; the man in Montana, $270,000. Many employees suing under any of the common law theories win significantly more money than that because most states permit juries to award you compensatory damages (money to cover your lost income), legal costs, *and* punitive damages (a sum of money intended to punish your employer for the wrongdoing). The punitive damages can run into the millions depending on how outrageous your employer's conduct was. And on top of all that, you'll be awarded your job back with all of its benefits.

Before you start hoping to be fired for a bad or illegal reason, remember that there is a downside. These cases take time— sometimes several years—and the process can be extremely frustrating and stressful. Furthermore, you might not win, in which case you could find yourself with a stack of legal bills and no job. If you find yourself in a situation where your common law employment rights may have been violated, speak to an attorney who's experienced in labor and employment law. He or she will give you an appraisal of your chances (for between $50 and $300 an hour), and, if you have a good case, might be willing to take it on "contingency." This means that you pay the attorney a percentage of your award (about one-third) if you win the case and nothing if you lose. This is often a good deal for you because it saves you money out of pocket and gives your attorney a strong motivation to fight hard for you.

Summary

For the purposes of review, it might be helpful to consider the predicament of our unemployed bartender. Recall that Jim was fired for refusing to serve alcohol to an intoxicated customer. What are his alternatives if he wants to get his job back? Can he rely on some of the common law options discussed in this chapter?

If the state he works in has a law against serving drunk customers, Jim could possibly make the case that he was fired in violation of public policy. He was terminated for refusing to break the law; in most states, an employer can't fire an employee for refusing to perform an illegal act. But even if the state doesn't have such a law, Jim could still argue that we as a nation have a general policy to discourage drunk driving. He could also look to his employee handbook (if one exists) for protection. If it says that Jim can only be fired for just cause or specifies any steps his employer must take before discharging an employee, Jim can build his case on that. The employer may have violated one of its own policies by abruptly firing him. Again, though, his success with this strategy will depend on legal opinion in the state in which he works.

Finally, if he works in one of those states that recognizes the implied covenant of good faith and fair dealing, he may be able to point to the employer's implied duty to treat him fairly. Or he may cite an incident where another bartender did the same thing but was not terminated.

Jim wouldn't have to go through all of these common law remedies if there were some simple law that said bartenders couldn't be discharged for refusing service (and, in fact, there is such a law in Utah). He could simply rely on that statute in his court battle. But you won't always find a law that specifically addresses your particular problem. And if you don't, the important thing to remember is this: if you're fired because you refused to do something illegal, or if you're fired for some other unfair reason, or if your employer breaks a promise when discharging you, even if your employer's action violates no statute, you may have grounds for a wrongful discharge case. When there's no statute to protect you, you might still have recourse through common law.

Other Common Questions about Wrongful Discharge

Q: Is there a law that says wrongful discharge is illegal?

A: Most of this chapter is devoted to discussing "common law" rules that pertain to wrongful discharge. These laws come from judges, not legislators, and are only applicable within that judge's jurisdiction. However, one state—Montana—does have a wrongful discharge law that protects employees in cases like those discussed in this chapter. Several other states are considering similar legislation at this time; eventually, many common law remedies may become obsolete.

Q: My employer recently made several changes to the employee handbook, most of which I didn't like. If it's considered a contract, why didn't the employees have any input?

A: Employers are free to change the contents of their handbook. Even though many states consider handbooks to be contracts, they're really one-way contracts that can be changed unilaterally by the employer. So if your employer suddenly puts in a disclaimer, or deletes the discipline and discharge page, that's generally legal.

8

Unions

After publicly firing three employees who started the drive for a union, the plant manager made an announcement. "I'll tell you what unions are all about!" the manager roared over the loudspeaker. "They're about striking, picketing, boycotts, violence, and corruption! They'll bleed a company dry and then, like your three disloyal friends here, none of you will have a job! If you know what's good for you, you'll tell this union to go to hell on election day!"

Unions are struggling to maintain both their membership and their reputation these days. It seems that the only time they attract any press is when they appear to be functioning contrary to the public interest. There's certainly more to the story though. Unions came into existence to protect workers from gross mistreatment by their employers, and to this day they generally work hard to protect members from exploitation and poverty.

If you're in a union, you probably know what I'm talking about. High wages, good benefits, reasonable hours, job security, fair treatment—you may have them all. Employment at will is a foreign concept to you because you have a written contract that clearly spells out the conditions for dismissal. But others of you may be dissatisfied with your union. Maybe you had to join and are required to pay dues against your wishes. Maybe you think the union treats you with less respect than your company ever did. Opinions on this point tend to vary greatly.

No matter what your opinion, it's essential that you know your rights. Even if you're not covered by a union contract, you should still be familiar with the law that allows you to join a union. This chapter advises you on your rights to organize a union, to participate in union activity, and to refrain from such activity.

Labor Law

Government regulation of the relationships among companies, unions, and union members is called "labor law." The **National Labor Relations Act** (NLRA) and its later amendments provide the federal framework for labor law in the private sector. Public employees are not protected by the NLRA but instead by individual state laws (described later in this chapter). Similarly, the NLRA excludes supervisors, managers, agricultural workers, domestic servants, independent contractors, and those covered by another labor law, the **Railway Labor Act** (for railroad and airline employees), from its coverage. If you don't fit into one of these categories, chances are that the NLRA protects your right "to form, join, or assist labor organizations . . . and to refrain from any and all such activity."

What specific rights does the NLRA offer you? The law says that your company cannot fire you, discipline you, or discriminate against you in any way for joining a union or for attempting to get a union to represent you and your coworkers. In other words, you have the right to start a union organizing drive and to solicit support from your fellow workers. If there's a significant amount of support for the union in your company, the union will ask the National Labor Relations Board (NLRB), the federal agency that administers the NLRA, to hold an election. The election is typically held at the company within two months of the request, and if more than 50 percent of the voting employees elect the union as their bargaining representative, the union wins. At this point, the law says that your company must bargain with the union over "wages, hours, and terms and conditions" of your employment.

Although this process sounds pretty cut and dry, it's not. In fact, much of the time the unionization process is not only complicated, it's downright ugly. Companies typically despise unions and will sometimes do whatever it takes to avoid unionization. Name calling, threats, promises, intimidation, coercion—the campaign leading up to a union election can make political campaigns look polite and cordial by comparison. This is one reason why labor law is so important. It protects you while taking part in activities that may not be popular with your boss.

It also protects your participation in union activities once the election is over and the union has been certified as your representative. You have the right to attend union meetings, to be a part of the negotiations team, to be a union steward, and to file grievances against the company without retaliation from your employer. In the private sector (and occasionally in the public sector) you also have the right to strike for a better contract or in response to "unfair labor practices" (see table 8.1) by your employer. But beware. Under the current law, if you go on strike to secure a more favorable contract, your company can permanently replace you or phase out your job. And don't kid yourself that this could never happen to you. Striker replacement has become a common tactic to weaken union support, to downsize, and to cut costs. Workers who resort to striking in today's business and legal climate are taking a risk.

As table 8.1 indicates, labor law also regulates the relationship between you and your union. Among the questions concerning unions most commonly asked by employees are: If the union wins, do I have to join? and Do I have to pay dues? The answers depend on (1) what has been negotiated between the union and the company and (2) what state you live in.

One of the first things that most unions will seek at the bargaining table is what's called a **"union security clause."** This provision, which may compel you to join the union, to pay dues to support it, or both, generally comes in three varieties:

Unions Shop Clause says that all employees that the union bargains for will becomes dues-paying members of the union within a specified period of time (usually thirty days).

Maintenance of Membership Clause does not compel membership as a condition of employment, but does require that all

TABLE 8.1
Unfair Labor Practices

An unfair labor practice (ULP) is defined as illegal interference with the rights granted to you in the NLRA. Listed below are some of the most commonplace actions that are typically found to be ULPs.

Employer ULPs

Discharging, disciplining, or discriminating against an employee because of that employee's union activities

Questioning employees about their views of the union in a coercive or threatening manner

Giving (or promising) employees an unscheduled wage increase or any gifts or job improvements while a union is trying to organize

Threatening to close the plant if the union wins the election

Threatening loss of jobs, wages, or benefits if employees vote for the union

Spying on employees who are participating in union activities

Preventing an employee from distributing union literature on nonwork time in nonworking areas

Making financial contribution to the union or dominating (controlling) it in any way

Refusing to bargain in good faith with the union

Union ULPs

Treating an individual employee or a group of employees in a discriminatory manner (including arbitrary or discriminatory refusal to process an employee's grievance)

Charging excessive dues or assessments (but periodic dues and initiation fees are legal)

Refusing to bargain in good faith with the employer

---

employees who become union members will remain members until the next contract.

Agency Shop Clause says that you are not required to join the union, but are required to pay union dues as a condition of employment. If you're not a union member and you object to the union's use of your dues for things that do not affect your employment, you need only pay that portion of dues that goes toward bargaining and contract administration (usually about 85 percent of regular dues). In other words, you don't have to finance any of the union's political activities, only those activities that directly benefit you. The union is required by law to inform nonmembers of this right each year.

Your ability to avoid union membership is therefore in part determined by which clause (if any) has been negotiated. It's also determined by where you live. Twenty-one states have outlawed most types of union security clauses altogether (see table 8.2). This means that if you work in one of these states, you typically cannot be obligated to join a union or to pay union dues against your wishes. Such legislation is called a "right to work" law and substantially weakens union power in those states.

The Duty of Fair Representation

As table 8.1 notes, unions are obliged by law to represent individual employees and employee groups fairly. But the boundaries of the union's so-called duty of fair representation (DFR) may surprise you.

Unions must treat all those for whom they bargain, both union members and nonmembers, black and white, women and men, equally. This applies to the handling of employee grievances, the negotiation of contract provisions, dues requirements, and all contract administration activities. So if a union refuses to handle your grievance because of your race, because you are not a member of the union, or because you have made derogatory statements about the union, it has committed an unfair labor practice by violating the DFR. The same is true if it were, for

TABLE 8.2
States with Right to Work Laws

Alabama	Kansas	South Carolina
Arizona	Louisiana	South Dakota
Arkansas	Mississippi	Tennessee
Florida	Nebraska	Texas
Georgia	Nevada	Utah
Idaho	North Carolina	Virginia
Iowa	North Dakota	Wyoming

instance, to negotiate a better wage for men than for women doing the same job.

Such blatant actions seldom happen though. More typically, unions have to respond to questions about why they didn't take an employee's grievance all the way to arbitration, or why they negotiated an affirmative action clause that seems to discriminate against whites and men. The law makes it very tough for an employee to win a case like this against a union. Unions are given *a lot* of leeway in deciding which grievances have merit and which contract clauses benefit the union as a whole. In other words, *the DFR does not hold unions to a very high standard of conduct.* Unless you have pretty clear evidence that the union discriminated against you (or your employee group) because of race, gender, religion, national origin, intraunion politics, nepotism, personal animosity, or nonmembership, or was grossly negligent in its representation of you, chances are that you won't get too far at the NLRB with a DFR charge. If the NLRB isn't receptive, you can attempt to sue your union in federal court for a breach of the DFR, but, again, such cases are very difficult to win. Often, what may appear to be "unfair" treatment is not considered unlawful treatment by the legal system.

Decertification of the Union

For those of you seeking to rid your company of unions altogether, the law provides one avenue, a "decertification" election. To initiate such an election, an employee must bring a petition to the NLRB that indicates that several employees no longer wish to be represented by the union. Such a petition can be as simple as, "We the undersigned wish to decertify the (union name) as our collective bargaining representative." This petition must be signed by at least 30 percent of the workers covered by the contract. Provided that the petition drive is started by one or more of these workers and is not motivated or assisted by management, the NLRB will hold a decertification election in your company. Remember, however, that the prounion forces discouraging decertification may be just as fierce as the antiunion forces that sought to derail the initial certification of the union. Although you're within your rights to undertake a decertification effort, be prepared for the potential backlash.

State and Local Employees

Because government workers' rights to unionize and to bargain are not protected by the NLRA, many states have passed laws to fill this void (see table 8.3) These laws apply only to state and local government employees. Most of the legislation looks very similar to the NLRA, providing rights to form, join, and assist unions; offering election procedures much like those described above; and outlawing unfair labor practices by public employees and unions. The agencies responsible for administering the laws are usually called the state "Public Employee Relations Board" (PERB) or "Public Employee Relations Committee" (PERC).

There are variations in procedures and rights across states and you should contact your state PERB or PERC for the specifics of

TABLE 8.3

States with Public-Sector Bargaining Laws

Alaska	Maryland	Ohio
Arizona*	Massachusetts	Oklahoma
California	Michigan	Oregon
Connecticut	Minnesota	Pennsylvania
Delaware	Missouri*	Rhode Island
Florida	Montana	South Dakota
Hawaii	Nebraska	Tennessee
Idaho	Nevada	Texas*
Illinois	New Hampshire	Vermont
Indiana	New Jersey	Washington
Iowa	New Mexico	West Virginia
Kansas	New York	Wisconsin
Maine	North Dakota	

*Professional public employees in Arizona, Missouri, and Texas have the right to "meet and confer" with the employer, but the employer is not obligated to actually bargain with them.

labor law in your state. There is also one big difference between public- and private-sector labor law: private-sector employees have the right to strike whereas public-sector employees typically do not. Not too fair considering the strike is the union's most potent weapon, right? Maybe, but would you want to see firefighters, police, sanitation workers, or teachers withholding their services in your town? Because public employees generally provide more vital services than do private-sector workers, only nine states (Alaska, Hawaii, Minnesota, Montana, Oregon, Pennsylvania, Rhode Island, South Dakota, and Vermont) grant public employees the right to strike. Even in most of these states, the right comes with some restrictions, and all but one (Montana) deny the right to strike to police and firefighters. Many states, however, provide for arbitration of contract disputes as an alternative to striking.

Federal Employees

Federal employees can look to the **Civil Service Reform Act** for their rights. Although federal workers can unionize, they have no right to strike and their right to bargain is very limited (for instance, they *cannot* bargain over wages, hours, and benefits, but they can bargain over grievance procedures and some work methods and technology issues). No doubt Congress really went all out on this one to make it look like it was protecting federal workers without actually doing so. In any case, the Federal Labor Relations Authority administers the Act and can be reached at 202-482-6560 if you want to know about things like the legality of bargaining over where your parking space will be located.

Summary

This brief chapter is only an introduction to a very complex area of the law. It's not intended to make you an expert, just to make you aware of your legal right to protect yourself *through* unionization and your right to *refrain from* unionization. Want more information? Each of the thirty-three regional offices of the NLRB and most PERB/PERC offices have agents available to answer your specific questions. Their phone numbers are in the blue pages of your telephone book.

Other Common Questions about Your Rights under Labor Law

Q: If I try to organize a union in my company and I get fired, or if I'm simply threatened for engaging in union activities, what do I do?

A: If you believe you were fired (or even threatened, disciplined, or discriminated against) because of your union activities, go to your nearest National Labor Relations Board regional office to file a complaint. An agent will take down the relevant information about your termination. A few days later another agent will help you prepare a signed and sworn statement (called an affidavit) detailing the incident and will then interview your employer (who will of course claim that you were fired for a legitimate reason).

How do they decide who's telling the truth? Usually the NLRB will look for five things in their investigation before agreeing to take your case before a judge: (1) union activity by you, (2) employer knowledge of your union activities, (3) employer hostility toward the union, (4) suspicious timing of the termination, and (5) different company treatment of you as compared to others. So if, for instance, you were a known union supporter, the company had made its opposition to the union clear, and you were fired during or soon after a union campaign for some reason that no one else is usually fired for, you stand a good chance that the NLRB will represent you to get your job back. Then it's up to the judge to decide. This entire process costs you no money.

Q: If the union wins, what issues get negotiated?

A: The NLRA says that the employer must bargain about "wages, hours, and terms and condition of employment." The last of these is a broad area that includes things like benefits, disciplinary procedures, job security, subcontracting, seniority provisions, and other issues that affect your work life. The company, however, reserves the right to set most hiring, firing, layoff, training, assignment, and other policies, and to make most work rules and strategic business decisions (financing, advertising, pricing, plant shutdown, and so on) by itself. Also, it's important to note that the company is not obligated to concede to any of the union's demands. The law only requires that it bargain "in good faith" (that is, in a sincere effort to reach agreement) on the issues outlined above.

In the public sector, what must be bargained varies by state. Generally, the law gives management a little more decision-making authority than it does in the private sector.

Q: If the union goes on strike, do I have to go on strike?

A: The union can't legally prevent you from crossing the picket line and continuing to work for your employer. It can, however, heavily fine union members who choose to work rather than support the strike.

Q: If I'm in a union, can I insist that my grievances be heard by an arbitrator?

A: You have the right to file grievances and to have your grievance considered by your union and management, but the union decides which grievances have enough merit to take to arbitration. As long as the union makes this decision solely on the basis of merit (their assessment of how winnable the grievance is) rather than on the basis of irrelevant considerations detailed in the "duty of fair representation" section of this chapter, the NLRB and the courts will defer to their judgment.

Q: How long do I have to file an unfair labor practice charge with the NLRB?

A: Once an incident has occurred that you suspect is an unfair labor practice, you have six months to file a charge.

EMPLOYEE
PRIVACY
AND
RELATED
ISSUES

9

General Privacy Issues

It was like something right out of 1984. Jen had walked into her new customer service job full of enthusiasm and excitement. During the orientation, though, she learned that it was common practice for the company to tap into her telephone conversations. Additionally, her supervisor would be monitoring not only her demeanor on the phone, but also the length of time to handle customer inquiries, the amount of time between calls, and how long she spent on break, at lunch, and in the bathroom.

C an your boss legally monitor your every move at work? Search your locker or desk? Scrutinize your off-duty conduct? Subject you to tests that reveal personal and sensitive information? In short, do you have to check your privacy rights at the door when you enter work each day?

The right to privacy is the right to be left alone. It is so highly valued in our society that you do have privacy rights at work, subject to some limitations. This section explains the boundaries of those rights. Specifically, this chapter covers searching employees, monitoring employees, and probing employees' off-duty lives. Chapters 10 and 11 examine employee testing issues, chapter 12 looks at employer statements about employees, and chapter 13 discusses your right to access your personnel file.

Can the Boss Search through Your Belongings?

Have you ever been infuriated because someone looked through your personal things without permission? If the boss is the one doing it, this act seems even more insidious. Surely there has to be some law that prevents this type of invasion.

This book discussed the concept of "common law" in chapters 2 and 7. You'll recall that precedents from court cases act as constraints on what your employer can do with respect to firing or disciplining you. Common law also grants you a limited right to privacy at work.

Each state has its own common law, so the extent to which you have privacy will vary according to where you work. In general, the law in most states says that if a "reasonable person" would find the employer intrusion into your personal belongings "highly offensive," and if you usually have an "expectation of privacy" at work, then the employer's search has probably violated your common law right to privacy. If you sift through the legal terms, this means: **If the average person (meaning one who isn't hypersensitive) would find the search shocking and intolerable, and if you normally expect that your belongings will remain private, then the search may be an illegal invasion of your privacy.**

"Highly offensive" is a self-explanatory term; however, "expectation of privacy" is a little more complex. An illustration should clarify the concept. The following incident actually happened in Texas:

A K-Mart department store issued lockers to all employees to use to store their personal items during working hours. It permitted employees to use their own locks if they wanted to, and many did. Among them was Billie Trotti. After someone had stolen merchandise, the company searched Trotti's locker without her consent, but did not find the stolen items.

Upon finding that her locker had somehow been opened and searched, Trotti sued K-Mart for invasion of privacy. The jury found that (1) a reasonable person would find the search highly offensive, and (2) that because Trotti had used her own lock, she had every reason to expect that the contents of her locker would remain private. The jury awarded her $108,000.

If K-Mart had issued its own locks and told employees that their lockers might be searched if necessary, would Trotti have won? Probably not because in that case Trotti would have had no reason to expect privacy. You need *both* a "highly offensive" intrusion and an "expectation of privacy" to win this type of privacy case.

Are You Being Watched?

Employee monitoring is an effective method of keeping employees from shirking. In the modern workplace there is no need for a supervisor to constantly watch over your shoulder, for the employer has high-tech methods to monitor your activities.

Making a personal phone call? Beware because your boss may be listening to it. Playing a computer game at work? Watch out because employers can monitor *everything* that's on your computer screen without you knowing it. Blowing off time talking to your coworkers? Make sure it's not caught on the surveillance camera.

Monitoring is intended to do more than simply prevent the "in-house vacation," though. Employers use it to assess performance, to identify training needs, and to deter theft. It can be a valuable management tool if used properly. Most employees, however, view monitoring as a devious and repugnant invasion of their privacy by a "Big Brother"–like boss.

Unfortunately for most of the estimated twenty-six million workers affected by monitoring, the majority of these supervising techniques are legal. If the employer has a legitimate reason to monitor you—for example, listening to the phone calls of telemarketers or evaluating the number of keystrokes you make per minute on your word processor—then there's little that you can do about it. Employers have a lot of leeway in the use of monitoring, but they are subject to some limitations.

Federal and state wiretapping laws, for example, allow your boss to listen in on your business-related telephone conversations but not on your personal calls. The boss can only eavesdrop on a personal call long enough to determine that it is indeed personal. After that point, your call can no longer legally be monitored.

Similarly, with surveillance cameras, your boss can only watch you when you're not engaged in private or personal matters. A camera can observe public areas like the office or the shop floor, the parking lot, or the lobby, but not, for instance, the bathroom. This is because employees expect privacy in some places but not in others.

Your common law right to privacy comes into play again here. Monitoring that reasonable people would find highly offensive isn't tolerated by the law. Most monitoring is legal, however, so that any employer who uses common sense while monitoring employees is on pretty safe ground.

Is Your Boss Prying into Your Off-Duty Conduct?

Your employer catches you stumbling out of a bar, or flipping through the adult movies section of the video store, or out on a date with a coworker. Can the employer fire you or demand that you alter your behavior? Isn't your off-duty time private and none of your employer's damn business?

Most of us would like to think so, but again it depends on where you work. Colorado, Nevada, North Dakota, and New York have laws prohibiting the discharge of an employee for legal off-duty conduct. Also, courts in states that recognize the implied covenant of good faith and fair dealing (discussed in chapter 7) would typically side with the employee on these issues. But courts in other states have permitted terminations that were prompted by an employee's social relationships, membership in controversial organizations like the KKK, or volunteer work with AIDS patients.

The bottom line: except in a handful of states, it is very difficult to predict how any individual case will be decided. In other words, we often don't know to what extent your boss can scrutinize your life away from work. A good rule of thumb is to use this book to determine the tenor of your state's employment laws. If they tend to be liberal (that is, proemployee), then you probably have a decent chance of keeping your boss out of your private life.

The Constitutional Right to Privacy

Do the U.S. and state constitutions give you a right to privacy? Yes. Does this right apply in your relationship with your employer? Not unless you're a public employee (or if you work in California, where the state constitution is considered to protect private-sector workers as well). Therefore, private-sector employees are generally unable to rely on the constitution for privacy rights at work.

Public employees' constitutional right to privacy at work will be balanced against their employer's need to supervise and maintain an efficient workplace. That means that employer searches, monitoring, or prying will be judged against the employer's need to do these things. If the employer doesn't have a good reason, its actions will probably be held unconstitutional. The next chapter presents a more detailed analysis of this point with specific attention to drug testing of public employees.

Summary

To fully understand the boundaries of your privacy rights at work, you'd probably have to read several books and maybe even take a law class. It's a complicated area with a long history of precedents. Therefore, it's important to recognize that this chapter has only provided a basic overview of those rights and of how most situations would be evaluated by a court.

In contrast to the situation with discrimination laws, there's no central agency to which you can go to obtain free legal advice and counsel on privacy rights. That means you have to hire your own attorney (or see your union representative) to pursue a case. That can be expensive, but the flip side is that you may win a lot in damages if you prove your case. As we've seen, however, that's a pretty big if.

10

Drug Testing

So one day your boss walks in and bluntly announces that a new corporate policy requires all employees to submit to screening for illegal drug use. A computer will periodically generate employee numbers at random and those workers will be drug tested or will lose their jobs for refusing. Thirty minutes later a handful of your coworkers are marched out the door. After a few days, two of them are terminated because their tests came up positive.

"Can they do this?!" you might ask in disbelief. "Test me for drugs any time they choose? Without warning? And then fire me if I don't pass?!" Generally, the answer in most private firms is yes, but . . .

Increasingly, employers are drug testing their workforces. Drug users are approximately three times more likely to have an accident, one-third as productive, and have much higher rates of tardiness and absenteeism than other workers. By many estimates, drug use among workers costs companies from $50 to $100 billion a year in lost man hours, damaged or destroyed equipment and product, increased insurance premiums, legal fees, and lost efficiency. As a result, many employers are fighting back by drug testing their workforces.

How Employee Drug Testing Works

A worker to be tested is typically escorted into a company bathroom, or in some cases to a medical facility, by an employer's representative of the same sex to produce a urine sample. The employee must show some type of identification, remove any coat or outer garment where a "confederate" (substitute) sample might be hidden, go into the stall to produce the sample, and provide the sample to the monitor. The monitor labels the sample with a bar code that confidentially links the sample to the employee, and sends it to a laboratory to be analyzed. The analysis accurately recognizes the presence of drugs in a person's system in about 99 percent of the cases.

Usually, any employee who tests positive for drug use is given a chance to offer an explanation for the result. A variety of over-the-counter cold medicines, some prescription medications, ibuprofen, and a host of other legal drugs can trigger a positive test result in the same way that illegal drugs do. These drugs are called "cross-reactants." If you can show that you have been taking some legal drug that corresponds to the illegal drug found in your bodily fluids, you'll probably be absolved of any wrongdoing.

By the way, if you eat a lot of poppy seed bagels, you will likely test positive for opiates. And if you regularly drink herbal teas made from coca leaves, don't be surprised if you're accused of using cocaine. These too are cross-reactants that look exactly the same to the laboratory as illegal drugs.

But what about the legality of drug testing? Can the employer really conduct them at will? **The bottom line: In the private sector, a company can drug test employees whenever it wants to unless there's a law or court case in its state that limits it from doing so.**

A company can require random drug testing of employees, applicant drug testing, drug testing during annual examinations, and "suspicion-based" drug testing—a situation where the employer has a particular reason to suspect that an individual employee uses drugs. Basically, in most states, if the company wants to drug test you, whether or not it has a good reason, it can do so.

Twelve states have laws that limit a company's free hand in drug testing employees. Usually a state law will merely require companies to ensure that they use proper procedures when testing employees, but three states (Minnesota, Connecticut, and Maine) limit drug testing to those workers whose drug impairment would pose some type of danger to themselves or those around them. A few, as noted in table 10.1, go so far as to outlaw random drug testing, only permitting suspicion-based tests. Additionally, courts in at leas four states (New Jersey, California, West Virginia, and Pennsylvania) have hinted that, even without a specific drug testing law, the state may have a public policy that protects workers—public and private—from being drug tested unless the employer has a good reason to do so (see chapter 7 for a further explanation of how state public policy protects workers).

Some workers have also tried to sue employers who seek to drug test them for violating what is called their "common law right to privacy" (see chapter 9). In plain English, this is a right that prohibits individuals from invading the privacy of other individuals. Although some workers have won a substantial amount of money in these cases, the cases are difficult to win and such awards are extremely rare.

Public-Sector Workers

Public-sector workers have additional protections. The U.S. and state constitutions not only regulate what the government can do with respect to its citizens, but also with respect to its employees. Specifically, the Fourth Amendment to the U.S.

TABLE 10.1
States that Limit Private-Sector Drug Testing

Connecticut**	Maine**	Nebraska
Hawaii	Maryland	Rhode Island*
Iowa*	Minnesota**	Utah
Louisiana	Montana*	Vermont*

*Iowa, Montana, Rhode Island, and Vermont outlaw random drug testing but permit suspicion-based drug testing.
**Connecticut, Maine, and Minnesota outlaw random drug testing unless the employee's position is "safety-sensitive."

Also, employers in Minnesota and Vermont cannot fire an employee for testing positive on the first offense unless the employee is unwilling to undergo employer-financed rehabilitation.

Constitution (and the corresponding clauses in state constitutions) prohibits the government from searching or ordering a search of a person's bodily fluids without a good reason to do so. This is a *constitutional* right to privacy, as distinguished from the common law right to privacy, and is generally available to employees of the federal, state, and local governments.

For the government to legally require drug testing, it must have a need to drug test that is so strong that this need outweighs an employee's constitutional right to privacy. These restrictions also apply when the government attempts to order testing of private-sector workers like airline pilots or railroad engineers.

To date, the courts have found that the government needs in testing pilots, air traffic controllers, prison guards, nuclear power plant operators, customs officials, army police, school bus drivers, and even airline flight attendants is sufficient to warrant drug testing, whether or not the individual to be tested is suspected of using drugs. **In a nutshell, if the employee is "safety-sensitive" (translation: serious consequences could occur if the employee were drug-impaired on the job), and if the government uses reasonable and accurate procedures to test, then the drug testing of public employees is usually legal.**

Summary

Returning to the workers in our opening section, what options do they have? If these are private-sector employees, we would want to know if the state they were in protected them from being randomly drug tested. If not, they still might be able to win a court case on the grounds that by demanding they surrender their bodily fluids for inspection, the company violated some state public policy that protects their privacy or violated their common law right to privacy.

If these are public-sector employees, they will have an easier road. In the public sector, only safety-sensitive employees can be drug tested at random. Unless the employer can show that drug impairment of these particular workers would directly lead to some type of calamity, the employer has violated these employees' constitutional right to privacy and would have to return the fired workers to their jobs.

Remember, though, that court cases are expensive, time-consuming, and can be quite stressful. Often, the best recourse is to first consider the specific state or constitutional protections available to you to see if the employer's policy violates your rights. If you cannot make a case this way, sometimes you only need to hint at a lawsuit (and sound like you know what you're talking about) to get the employer to reconsider its drug-testing policy.

Terminology of Drug Testing

Sample   A urine specimen used to identify the presence of any drugs in the employee's system

Random Drug Testing   The practice of arbitrarily selecting workers to be drug tested

Suspicion-Based Testing   Drug testing an individual only upon having some reason to believe that the individual uses illegal drugs

Positive Test   When a sample is identified as containing evidence of illegal drug use

False Positive   When a sample is incorrectly identified as a positive because of the slight inaccuracy of the test

Cross-Reactant   A legal substance that shows up as an illegal drug in the urine

Chain of Custody Form   A form that accompanies the employee's sample to confidentially identify whom the sample belongs to and where it was from the time it was produced to the time it was analyzed

Safety-Sensitive   A term used to denote workers whose drug impairment would directly lead to some danger or harm

Other Common Questions about Drug Testing

Q: Do I have to submit to drug testing when applying for a job?
A: It is generally acknowledged by most courts that applicants expect to disclose personal information to get a job. Because of this, private-sector employers can almost always, if they so

choose, require that applicants pass a drug test as a condition of employment. Two notable exception: (1) private-sector employers in Montana can only test applicants for "safety-sensitive" positions, and (2) applicant testing in Iowa must be part of a general physical exam.

Applicants for public-sector employment should only have to submit to drug testing if their jobs meet the "safety-sensitive" criterion discussed in this chapter.

Q: What drugs do the laboratories look for?

A: The most common tests screen for alcohol, marijuana, cocaine, amphetamines, barbiturates, opiates, PCP, LSD, morphine, heroin, or any combination of these.

Q: Will I test positive for drug use if I was simply in the same room as someone who was smoking marijuana?

A: Right now, the answer to this question is still disputed. According to the best information available, you will likely have traces of marijuana in your body for a day or two but the level will be extremely low. Some labs will report such small traces as positives but others will not.

If you test positive for this reason, be sure to inquire about the "cutoff level" for a positive test when offering your alternative explanation for the result. If the cutoff is near 20 nanograms per milliliter of urine, your explanation is plausible. If it's closer to 100 nanograms, they probably won't believe you. (Don't worry if this sounds too technical—if you've really tested positive because of passive inhalation and you use this information, you'll probably blow your boss away *and* you may save your job.)

Q: If I am represented by a union, can the employer *still* require that I take a drug test?

A: Again, there's a distinction between the public and private sectors. Currently, if there's no language in the union contract that covers drug testing, public employers are generally free to develop their own policies (subject, of course, to the constitutional limitations outlined in this chapter). Private-sector employers must bargain with the union over any plan to drug test those covered by the contract before any testing can occur.

Q: Besides drug usage, can the tests tell anything else about me from my sample?

A: Yes! This is one of the biggest objections that people have to drug testing. Your bodily fluids reveal things like pregnancy, epilepsy, diabetes, and other information you may want to keep private. As a result, many employers and labs are careful to provide assurances that they will only screen for illegal drug use.

11

Other Tests for Employees

Seldom had David felt such anxiety when taking a test. He figured that landing a security guard job after high school would be simple—he was big, he was intimidating, and he even made the all-state wrestling team in his senior year. He was prepared for anything. Until, that is, he ran into questions like "Have you ever indulged in unusual sexual practices?," "Are you attracted to members of the same sex?," and "Do you have any strong religious beliefs?" on the company's written employment test.

Recently, a jury in California awarded $2 million to a group of job applicants who were forced to answer these and other sensitive questions to be considered for employment. The employment test was unfair. The questions were irrelevant. The privacy rights of the applicants were violated. Apparently the jurors, many of whom were themselves employees, never wanted to confront such a test. In no uncertain terms, they sent a message to employers in the state of California (and elsewhere) that employment testing has boundaries.

A written test, a lie detector test, an AIDS test, or any other type of test required by your employer (or prospective employer) is usually intended to gauge your competency or worthiness to perform a particular job. Some tests do this very well, others do not. This chapter will advise you on the legality of different employment tests.

Written and Physical Tests

Depending on the jobs you've applied for or the promotions you've sought, you may have had to take some sort of employment test. Typically, the experience is nerve-racking because so much seems to be on the line. Why do such tests exist? Because a lot is on the line for employers too. They need methods to predict your future performance, especially if they intend to invest time, money, and other resources in training you. Informal interviews can provide them with only some of the information they would like to have. Properly developed tests can often provide them with much more.

But an employer faces a tough choice in deciding whether to test. Those who don't test risk hiring unqualified individuals, which can be very costly. Some who do test hire a professional test designer to construct a "properly developed" test, which is also costly. Not surprisingly, many employers choose to create their own employment tests in an effort to save money. The irony is that this may be the most costly option of all. As we've seen, the consequences of asking job applicants questions that have no direct relation to the position they're seeking could cost as much as $2 million.

If you are required to take a test that doesn't accurately predict how you will do in a particular job or one that expects you to divulge information that is personal and/or irrelevant, you could take the employer to court with a very good chance of winning. In other words, if an employer asks David about his "sexual practices" or "religious beliefs" on a test to determine his ability to perform as a security guard, the employer would have legal problems unless it could prove that these questions were somehow "job-related." In this case, the employer couldn't.

In the same way, the law scrutinizes tests that have a tendency to screen out people by race, sex, religion, national origin, age, or disability. Take, for example, a fitness test that requires applicants for a warehouse job to demonstrate the ability to lift and carry a seventy-five-pound box. Such a test would undoubtedly screen out more women than men. But this fact alone would not make the test unlawful. If lifting and carrying heavy boxes is a regular and necessary part of the warehouse job, the test should be a good indicator of future job performance and is probably legal (see "disparate impact" discrimination, discussed in chapter 3). However, if heavy lifting is not common in this job, the test amounts to a form of gender discrimination and violates the law. **The bottom line: a written or physical employment test is considered lawful if the employer can prove that the test is job-related and that the test accurately predicts job performance.**

HIV/AIDS Tests

Tests of physical fitness sometimes go well beyond lifting a box. Although AIDS cannot be transmitted through normal work activities, employers concerned about health risks to their work-force and about their insurance costs are increasingly testing job applicants for HIV. Consequently, they're also increasingly finding themselves in court.

This area of the law is a little complicated and is still developing, but it's becoming reasonably clear when HIV testing is and is not permissible. The **Americans with Disabilities Act** (see chapter 4) prohibits an employer from testing for HIV and other health conditions before it makes a job offer. HIV testing of job applicants (as long as all applicants are tested) is permitted after a job offer is made and before employment actually begins. The information obtained from such a test, with very few exceptions, must be kept confidential.

Hawaii, Illinois, Kentucky, Massachusetts, New Mexico, Rhode Island, Texas, and Wisconsin have gone further than this by explicitly outlawing HIV testing by employers. Some other states (at present, Delaware, Iowa, Maine, Missouri, Oregon, and West Virginia) have broad laws restricting HIV testing which do not single out employers, but in all likelihood do apply to them.

Even in states where applicants can be tested, employers can almost never test current employees for HIV. To justify this form of testing, an employer would have to prove a business necessity for testing—for example, that there is a substantial risk of transmission of the disease. Given what we now know about how AIDS is transmitted, establishing a business necessity for testing may be virtually impossible.

Public-sector employers have additional obstacles: the U.S. and state constitutions. As in the case of drug testing (discussed in chapter 10), the public-sector employer must show that the need to test you is so great that it outweighs your constitutional right to privacy. Only where there is a genuine risk of AIDS transmission by exposure to blood (with firefighters, for instance) might a public employer be able to defend the practice of HIV testing.

Lie Detector (Polygraph) Tests

The law is very clear here. The **Employee Polygraph Protection Act (EPPA)** makes it illegal for most private-sector employers to perform a lie detector test or even to request that you take one as an applicant or as an employee. **You cannot be denied employment, or discharged, or discriminated against for refusal to take a polygraph test.**

There are only a handful of exceptions. If, for example, an employer is investigating a specific theft, you had access to the money or property that was stolen, and the employer has a good reason to believe that you took it, then you can be tested provided the employer gives you forty-eight hours written notice of the test. Other exceptions exist for security employees who handle money or classified information, and for applicants for pharmaceutical jobs who would have access to controlled substances. Otherwise, private-sector employees are protected from polygraph examinations.

The EPPA does not apply to public-sector employers. This does not mean that federal, state, and local government employers can require employees to submit to lie detector tests at will, though. Many public employees are protected through state laws. Eight states outlaw polygraph testing of public employees (Hawaii, Massachusetts, Michigan, Minnesota, Montana, Nevada, New York, and Oregon) and fourteen others and the District of Columbia permit only narrow exceptions to this rule (Alaska, California, Connecticut, Delaware, Maine, Maryland, Nebraska, New Jersey, Pennsylvania, Rhode Island, Vermont, Washington, West Virginia, and Wisconsin). Typically, the exceptions are police and/or those who handle dangerous substances or narcotics.

Even in states without a polygraph law, public employers are still limited by that nagging problem posed by the constitution and public employees' rights to privacy. As a result, public employees cannot be asked or required to undergo a polygraph examination unless the employer has a "legitimate need" to test—in other words, if significant harm could result from putting someone who's dishonest or prone to deviant behavior in a sensitive position (for example, in a police department or in an agency that handles classified information). Therefore, if you're a public employee who's not in one of the states with a polygraph law, you can still rely on the U.S. or your own state constitution for possible protection from lie detector tests.

Honesty and Psychological Tests

The EPPA all but eliminates the employer's ability to conduct lie detector tests. But employers still have a need to determine whether applicants and current employees are honest and psychologically fit to perform their jobs. One option they have is to check an applicant's references, but, as chapter 12 indicates, fewer and fewer employers will provide information about former employees to a prospective employer for fear that those former employees will sue them for damaging their reputation. So what is an employer to do?

Paper-and-pencil honesty tests (also called integrity tests) are becoming increasingly popular because they furnish employers with some of the information they desire. These tests purport to measure a person's potential for theft, tardiness, and absenteeism, and their likelihood of engaging in a strike. **The EPPA does not prohibit the use of honesty tests and only two states, Massachusetts and Rhode Island, restrict their use.** Therefore, it is generally legal for an employer to test you in this way. However, it has not yet been proven that these tests are valid; that is, it isn't known whether they indeed measure honesty and so the employer's reliance on these tests may soon be challenged successfully in court. This area of the law is just developing, but it is expected that employers will eventually be required to demonstrate that—just like other employee tests—honesty tests are valid and that they are related to the job. Also, employers will almost certainly be required to keep the results of an honesty test confidential.

Psychological tests, by contrast, have been validated and can accurately measure things like psychopathic behavior, loss of judgment under stress, whether a person handles criticism well, and whether a person is a danger to others. In other words, they offer information that employers surely would like to have concerning their applicants and employees. Here again, these tests are not illegal under the EPPA or under any state law. They are almost always considered legal if the information they provide is related to the job and if the results are kept confidential.

Summary

Similar to the decision in the California case, a jury in Maine recently awarded $960,000 to a police officer who was suspended for refusing to take a test that measured sexual arousal patterns. Even though cases like these are relatively rare, they demonstrate that when employer stupidity reaches new heights, so do jury verdicts. These cases mean that your boss and your future bosses have been put on notice: test applicants and employees unfairly and risk losing a lawsuit.

Because the law in this area is still evolving, there is no way to predict with certainty which tests will violate the law. Are psychological tests valid? What about genetic tests? Or honesty tests? There's a whole array of new questions that will eventually be answered by judges, juries, and legislators. However, the emerging trend indicates that employers must be able to justify any and all forms of testing. Therefore, if you are forced to take a test that seems to have no relation to your job, or one that appears to discriminate against a protected group, you well may have yourself a winnable case.

But if you really want the job and would like to save yourself time and aggravation, you may want to consider politely sharing your concern with your boss before you consult with an attorney. Given the current legal climate, he or she may be more receptive than you'd think!

12

Defamation of Employees

Pat was fired for sexually harassing a coworker. Even though the company had no real evidence, they decided to make an example of him to demonstrate their conviction on the issue. In fact, Pat was innocent of the charges.

For over six months now, Pat has been interviewing for jobs without any luck. Apparently, when prospective employers call his former boss for a reference, they learn why he was fired. As a result, he's promptly eliminated from further consideration.

We wouldn't feel bad for Pat if he were guilty of sexual harassment. He'd deserve what he was getting. But in this case, Pat's reputation has been ruined by his former company without justification. False information from his old boss is jeopardizing his livelihood and career. Fortunately, for Pat and anyone else in similar circumstances, there is legal recourse.

When Person A provides false information about Person B to Person C, and that information harms the reputation of Person B, then Person B can sue Person A for "defamation." Regarding Pat and his predicament, he can sue his old company because its communication of a false or misleading statement so damaged Pat's reputation that he couldn't find employment.

Defamatory statements can be in either written or oral form; the former is called "libel," the latter is called "slander." In the workplace context, both arise most often when employers provide references or when employers tell their workforces why a particular employee was fired.

Defamation in References

Have you noticed how many employers are refusing to give references these days? It's because they're terrified of defamation suits—as well they should be. Employees are filing more of these actions than ever before and some, like a California man who was awarded almost $1 million because of the defamatory references provided by his former employer, obtain huge settlements.

To prove his case, Pat needs to demonstrate that (1) a false statement by his employer (2) was communicated to a third party, and (3) harmed his reputation such that he could not find work. If he can do that, a jury, most of whom are probably workers themselves, may decide that his former employer should compensate him for lost earnings ("compensatory" damages). The jury may also order the employer to pay *a lot more* as punishment for its actions ("punitive" damages). This is what scares employers, and this is why fewer are providing references.

Communicating Why an Employee Was Fired

The company wanted to make an example of Pat. Suppose, then, that management called all its workers to a meeting and announced that "Pat was fired for sexual harassment and anyone else who exhibits similar behavior will also be terminated!"

Such a public announcement could be a pretty strong deterrent. It could serve a very important and legitimate purpose, especially if harassment was prevalent in the company. If the statements about Pat were true and were simply motivated by employer concern for proper employee conduct, then no defamation has occurred. If the statements are not true, however, Pat's reputation has been unjustifiably damaged and he has grounds for a case.

Summary

Employers are permitted to make truthful statements about employees and former employees to those seeking references and to current employees who have a legitimate interest in the information. They get into trouble when they lie, offer insupportable conclusions, or maliciously misrepresent individuals in a way that results in the loss of the individual's reputation. The smart employer will not report *conclusions* about employees (like "he sexually harassed a colleague"), only *accurate facts* (like "a woman accused him of harassment, so we let him go"). Unfortunately, many employers don't understand this distinction. If your boss is one of them and has unfairly damaged your good name, a trip to your attorney's office may be in order.

Other Questions about Employee Defamation

Q: If my boss yells at me in front of my coworkers, can I sue for defamation?

A: Usually not. But it really depends on a few things: the accuracy of the statement, the motivation for the statement, and the harm caused by the statement.

Accuracy: Did your boss say something that you think is blatantly untrue about you? For instance, did he call you "lazy" or "stupid" in front of others? The accuracy of the statement is important. If he's just stating things that are factual, like "You've been absent six times this month!" or "You're consistently the slowest worker on this team!," then your defamation suit probably won't win you anything but more headaches at work.

Motivation: Motive can also be an important ingredient of a defamation suit. If the motive for chewing you out is improper, for example, because of your race or because your boss is trying to force you to quit, then he's on dangerous ground. Bosses who reprimand employees for legitimate disciplinary reasons, on the other hand, are typically not violating the law.

Harm: Did you suffer any real harm from the statements? The law requires you to demonstrate that your reputation was damaged as part of a defamation suit.

The bottom line is that if your boss makes a false statement about you in front of others and/or maliciously undermines your reputation, you may have a case.

Q: I can't get a job without telling the interviewer the bogus reason they fired me. Even though it's not my former boss communicating this information, I'm still being harmed because I can't find work!

A: Actually, you may still have a defamation case even though your boss tells *no one* why you were fired. Courts in a growing number of states have ruled that if you're forced to restate the reason given for your termination, if that reason is insupportable or false, and if some harm comes to you because of it, your old company may still be liable. Remember, though, this only applies if you're not guilty of the actions for which you were fired.

13

Access to
Your Personnel File

After his suspension for fighting, Dan became curious. Was the company slowly building a case so they could eventually fire him? He recalled that each time he had been late, his supervisor would jot something down on his clipboard. The same was true when he carelessly dented the forklift. Just what kind of information did the company have in his file? Dan requested to see his personnel records. He was flatly denied.

Want to see your personnel file? In many states, you can, but in many others, you may not have this right. State **"Freedom of Information"** (FOI) laws permit employees to inspect most of the records kept on them by their employers. You may want to ensure that everything in your file is correct, you may want copies of some medical records, or you might just be curious about the file's contents. Regardless of the reason, where you live determines if you are entitled by law to access these records.

The Ground Rules

States with FOI laws are listed in table 13.1. To access your records, you must first provide your employer with a written request. Within a reasonable period of time (usually seven work

TABLE 13.1

States with Employee Record Access Laws

Alaska	Massachusetts	Pennsylvania
Arizona*	Michigan	Rhode Island
California	Minnesota	South Dakota*
Connecticut	Nebraska*	Tennessee*
Delaware	Nevada	Texas***
Dist. of Columbia**	New Hampshire	Utah*
Illinois	North Carolina**	Vermont*
Iowa	North Dakota	Washington
Kentucky*	Oregon	Wisconsin
Maine		

*Law applies to public employees only.
**Law applies to state (or D.C.) employees only.
***Texas law applies to public safety employees only.

days), your employer must show you your file. Typically, this will take place during nonworking hours.

Often, the employer can insist on being present when you inspect the file. You'll probably find information on payroll, taxes, benefits, safety incidents, and your qualifications in there. You might also see performance appraisals and disciplinary records. What you should not find is anything that isn't job-related (personal information, credit checks, and so on). Your employer has to have a legitimate business reason to keep each piece of information on you.

Many states permit you to see your file one or two times per year. If you find any inaccuracies, the law often provides specific procedures to follow to correct or to challenge the false information. Say, for instance, you find a disciplinary warning stating that you were reprimanded for swearing at your supervisor. You've told management repeatedly, however, that you were provoked, but that part of the story isn't in the disciplinary record. To set the record straight for anyone who sees the file in the future, you can request that the warning be amended to reflect both sides. Or you can submit your own explanation on a separate sheet of paper to be included in the file. In any case, it's a good idea to be sure that disciplinary and all other information is entirely accurate.

Medical Records

Employees in all fifty states have access to their medical records kept by their employers thanks to the **Occupational Safety and Health Act.** This federal law, discussed in detail in chapter 22, also allows you to make copies of the records and to see employer data concerning your exposure to harmful workplace substances.

Similarly, federal legislation protects the confidentiality of your medical file. Under the **Americans with Disabilities Act** (ADA), employers with fifteen or more employees must now keep information on your medical history and current medical condition in a separate personnel file. The only people legally allowed access to this file—other than you and the personnel manager who keeps the records—are your supervisor (but only if your condition requires a special accommodation), medical personnel (if your condition may require emergency attention), and government officials who are confirming that your employer is in compliance with ADA guidelines. Otherwise, your medical records are private.

Summary

Most states do not have FOI laws that apply to everyone, so there is a high probability that your employer can legally deny you access to your personnel records. But you cannot be prohibited from viewing your medical records. If you get an opportunity to review some or all of your records, take a careful look through whatever is provided to you. Check to see that there's nothing irrelevant or unrelated to business needs. Check the accuracy of your benefits records, including vacation time, health insurance plans, and pension contributions. Most importantly, check to make sure that all the information is correct, especially if you've been disciplined.

WAGES
AND
HOURS

14

Employee Wages

Mary Anne knew that bagging groceries wasn't her true calling, but she needed the money for college and she had few job choices. After receiving her first paycheck, she noticed the number 3.35 in the "Hourly Rate" column. Being a perceptive teen, she recognized the error and politely pointed out to the store manager that minimum wage was now $4.25 an hour. Her manager just chuckled, folded her arms, and said, "Listen, honey. When you're worth $4.25, you'll get $4.25. Now get back to work!"

Money is the primary reason most of us work. We have to pay the mortgage, buy food and clothing, put gas in the car, and purchase a million other things. We'd even like to buy a luxury now and then. The last thing we need after putting in our time is a complication with our paycheck.

Employers can easily exploit their employees' dependency on pay. They may dock your wages, they may refuse to pay you for unproductive time, or they may pay you less than they pay someone else simply because of your race or gender. Pay is an important source of power for employers and we would like to ensure that this power isn't abused.

Federal Law

Many wage and work hour laws have been passed in the United States but the most significant one, enacted by Congress in

1938, is the **Fair Labor Standards Act** (FLSA). The Act sets the minimum wage and overtime premium, regulates child labor, and guarantees that men and women will be paid equally for equal work. The basics of the FLSA and of other wage laws are discussed here. Later, chapters 15 and 16 will address the issues of overtime, child labor, and equal pay.

Before considering how the FLSA works, an important first question to ask is "Does the law apply to me?" Usually, the answer is yes, but there are several exceptions.

Almost all employers, state and local governments as well as private employers, must abide by the provisions of the FLSA. In fact, the law is currently designed to cover as many employers as possible. However, local businesses (technical definition: those who gross less than $500,000 a year or who do less than $50,000 in interstate business) are not covered by the FLSA, but instead by state regulations. In practical terms, this means that they can ignore the federal minimum wage standard, the overtime premium, and other provisions of the FLSA, but they still must comply with similar laws passed by their state government.

Even if your employer is covered by the FLSA, you may not be. You've probably heard the terms "nonexempt employee" and "exempt employee" around your workplace. These terms refer to whether a particular worker is covered (nonexempt) or not covered (exempt) by the FLSA. **Generally, most blue-collar employees and most pink-collar employees (for example, clericals, waitresses) are covered by the FLSA whereas most white-collar employees are not.**

In particular, the FLSA does not apply to "executives" (those primarily engaged in management and who supervise at least two other employees), "professionals" (those paid to use their knowledge, creativity, and judgment), "administrators" (those who perform office or nonmanual work related to management policy and who generally exercise discretion), or "outside salespeople" (those who spend at least 80 percent of their worktime in sales and who predominantly do business outside the workplace). It also does not protect most agricultural employees, camp employees, domestic companions, messengers, news delivery people, and a few other categories of workers described in the minimum wage and overtime sections of this book. Oh, and by the way, all you babysitters who get food thrown at you for three bucks an hour, you're not covered either.

Minimum Wage

The federal minimum wage is $4.25 per hour. This means that employers, with the exceptions detailed below, cannot pay you less than this amount. Many states have their own minimum wage law, some requiring that employers pay more than $4.25.

What's your hourly wage? To calculate it, simply divide your pay this week (before taxes) by the number of hours you worked this week. If that number is less than 4.25, you'll want to pay close attention to the next few pages.

Not all employers are required to pay the minimum wage. Anyone who's ever been a waiter or waitress knows this truth all too well. That's because "tipped" employees (those who receive more than $30.00 per month in tips and who get to keep all their tips) need only be paid half the minimum wage, or $2.13 per hour. This same rule applies even if tips are "pooled" and then split among several employees.

Other employees who don't have to be paid the minimum wage by law are listed in table 14.1. These include those receiving meals and lodging from their employer, cleaners of private homes, and

TABLE 14.1

Workers Who Do Not Have to Be Paid
the Federal Minimum Wage

- Waiters, waitresses, and other tipped employees
- Independent contractors (people like consultants, analysts, realtors, and outside salespersons)
- Cleaners of private homes
- Babysitters
- Employees receiving meals or lodging from their employer
- Employees in the knitted wear, hosiery, glove, and cigar industries
- Employees whose employers are too small to be covered under the FLSA

"independent contractors" (a whole class of workers to be defined later in this chapter). "Special" (that is, lower) minimum wages exist for employees in the apparel, knitted-wear, hosiery, glove, and cigar industries. Almost everyone else's pay cannot go below the federal minimum of $4.25 an hour.

Except, that is, unless your employer is one of the very few not covered by the FLSA. However, even most of these small employers are still subject to state minimum wage legislation.

Table 14.2 displays the minimum wage for each state. A handful of states (Alaska, Connecticut, the District of Columbia, Hawaii, Iowa, New Jersey, and Oregon) exceed the $4.25 threshold set by the FLSA. Employers in these states, therefore,

TABLE 14.2
State Minimum Wages

Alaska $4.75	Maine $4.25	Ohio $4.25
Arkansas $4.25	Maryland $4.25	Oklahoma $4.25
California $4.25	Massachusetts $4.25	Oregon $4.75
Colorado $3.00	Michigan $3.35	Pennsylvania $4.25
Connecticut $4.27	Minnesota $4.25	Rhode Island $4.45
Delaware $4.25	Missouri $4.25	South Dakota $4.25
Dist of Col $4.85	Montana $4.25	Texas $3.35
Georgia $3.25	Nebraska $4.25	Utah $4.25
Hawaii $5.25	Nevada $4.25	Vermont $4.25
Idaho $4.25	New Hampshire $4.25	Virginia $4.25
Illinois $4.25	New Jersey $5.05	Washington $4.25
Indiana $3.35	New Mexico $4.25	West Virginia $4.25
Iowa $4.65	New York $4.25	Wisconsin $4.25
Kansas $2.65	North Carolina $4.25	Wyoming $1.60
Kentucky $4.25	North Dakota $4.25	

There is no minimum wage law in Alabama, Arizona, Florida, Louisiana, Mississippi, or Tennessee.

South Carolina sets a minimum wage of $4.25 for machine shop and textile mill workers for Sunday work.

Minimum wages below $4.25 are only applicable to workers whose employers are not covered by the FLSA.

must comply with the state minimum rather than with the federal minimum.

If your employer is covered by the FLSA, the minimum wage that is applicable to you is $4.25 or the state minimum, *whichever is greater.* Is your hourly wage this week at or above the minimum you are due? If not, you're not alone. The FLSA is probably the most violated of all employment laws. If you believe that your employer is paying you below minimum wage, you can contact your state labor department (see Appendix A) or the Wage and Hour Division of the U.S. Department of Labor for help. If you have a valid claim, a representative from one of these departments will pursue the matter with your employer. Those who win their cases can receive reasonable attorney fees and costs in addition to *double* what they are owed in back wages.

Other Wage Legislation

State wage regulations go far beyond simply setting a minimum wage, though. Almost every state has a law that specifies how often an employee must be paid, in what form an employee must be paid (for example, in cash or by check), and what types of pay deductions and garnishments are permitted.

Let's say your boss tells you that doing the weekly payroll has become such a burden on the personnel staff that henceforth the company will issue paychecks every other month. This switch from fifty-two to six pay periods will save your employer a lot of administrative costs and will help the personnel department to run more efficiently. Your next paycheck will be available in two months.

Okay, so this is unfair and ridiculously poor management. But is it legal? In most states, the answer is no. Everywhere except Alabama, Florida, and South Carolina, most employees must be paid at least every thirty-five days. In all likelihood, as table 14.3 shows, you're probably owed a paycheck much more frequently than this.

Additionally, your employer is required to pay you in cash or in an easily cashed instrument such as a check or a money order. In most states, direct deposit is also an acceptable alternative.

TABLE 14.3
Maximum Interval between Paychecks

Alaska	monthly or twice a month, at the employee's option
Arizona	twice a month, not more than sixteen days apart
Arkansas	twice a month; monthly for executive and managerial employees
California	twice a month; monthly for executives and managerial employees
Colorado	monthly
Connecticut	weekly
Delaware	monthly
District of Columbia	twice a month
Georgia	twice a month
Hawaii	twice a month
Idaho	monthly
Illinois	twice a month
Indiana	twice a month
Iowa	monthly
Kansas	monthly
Kentucky	twice a month
Louisiana	every two weeks
Maine	within eight days of earning the wages
Maryland	twice a month
Massachusetts	every two weeks
Michigan	monthly if paid by the first of the month; if twice a month, payment due by first and fifteenth of the month
Minnesota	monthly
Mississippi	twice a month for employers of fifty or more employees
Missouri	twice a month
Montana	within ten business days after the end of the employer's pay period
Nebraska	regularly, by agreement of employer and employee
Nevada	at least the first or fifteenth of the month
New Hampshire	within eight days of the end of the employer's pay period

TABLE 14.3 *(Continued)*
Maximum Interval between Paychecks

New Hampshire	within eight days of the end of the employer's pay period
New Jersey	twice a month; monthly for executive and supervisory employees
New Mexico	twice a month; monthly for white-collar employees
New York	weekly for manual workers; twice a month otherwise
North Carolina	monthly
North Dakota	twice a month
Ohio	monthly if paid by the first of the month; if twice a month, payment due by first and fifteenth of the month
Oklahoma	twice a month
Oregon	every thirty-five days
Pennsylvania	within fifteen days of the end of the employer's pay period
Rhode Island	weekly within nine days of end of the employer's pay period for nonsalaried employees
South Carolina	weekly for textile workers; no maximum interval for other workers
South Dakota	monthly
Tennessee	twice a month, due by the fifth and twentieth of each month
Texas	twice a month
Utah	twice a month
Vermont	weekly; twice monthly if employees are given written notice
Virginia	twice a month for hourly employees; monthly for salaried employees
Washington	monthly
West Virginia	every two weeks
Wisconsin	monthly
Wyoming	twice a month, due on the first and fifteenth

State laws also dictate what can and can't be deducted from your pay. As you're no doubt painfully aware, federal and state income taxes, Social Security tax, and unemployment insurance contributions are legal deductions. You may also find union dues and your contributions to health insurance, pension, and other such benefits taken out of your pay. Your employer cannot deduct expenses for work-related injuries, for employer-mandated medical exams, or for losses due to customer thefts and breakages.

"Garnishments" (money taken out of your wages for the payment of your debts) may also be legally withheld. If you owe child support, for instance, a court may order a portion of your wages garnished until your debt has been paid. But your entire paycheck *cannot* be withheld. Table 14.4, designed by the U.S. Department of Labor, illustrates exactly how much of your after-deduction earnings can be garnished.

Again, if you believe your rights have been violated with respect to any of these pay issues, the appropriate place to go is to your state labor department.

Independent Contractors

One group of workers not protected by the FLSA are known as independent contractors. To determine if a worker is an inde-

TABLE 14.4
Garnishment of Wages*

Weekly Wage	Biweekly Wage	Semimonthly Wage	Monthly Wage
$127.50 or less: NONE	$255.00 or less: NONE	$276.25 or less: NONE	$552.50 or less: NONE
Between $127.50 and $170.00: AMOUNT ABOVE $127.50	Between $255.00 and $340.00: AMOUNT ABOVE $255.00	Between $276.50 and $368.55: AMOUNT ABOVE $276.50	Between $552.50 and $736.67: AMOUNT ABOVE $552.50
$170.00 or more: MAXIMUM OF 25%	$340.00 or more: MAXIMUM OF 25%	$368.55 or more: MAXIMUM OF 25%	$736.67 or more: MAXIMUM OF 25%

*The way to read this chart is as follows:
1. Locate the column that represents how often you receive a paycheck: weekly, biweekly (every two weeks), semimonthly (twice a month), or monthly.
2. Locate the cell in that column that represents how much you earn in that period **after deductions**.
3. The boldfaced type indicates how much of your wage can be garnished.

pendent contractor, the law takes into account several aspects of the relationship between worker and employer. Does the employer schedule the worker's hours? Does the employer provide training for the worker? To what extent does the employer direct the activities of the worker? Are the duties of the worker routine or do they require some degree of specialization? Does the worker invest in his or her own equipment and facilities? Does the worker rely on the employer for his or her livelihood?

There is, at present, no hard-and-fast rule for defining an independent contractor. Usually, no one feature of the relationship will by itself determine the status of the worker. Instead, the law looks at the whole relationship to ascertain how much control the employer exercises over the worker and how dependent the worker is on the employer for training, supervision, and wages. The closer the relationship, the more likely the worker is really an employee and not a contractor.

Summary

There are few investigations that scare an employer more than a wage audit by the U.S. Department of Labor. This is because if the employer is found to have improperly paid one employee, the employer is probably guilty of improperly paying dozens, perhaps hundreds, of similar employees. If the mistake is an honest one, the penalty is typically double what was owed to all employees plus payment of the lawyers for both sides—in other words, potentially a lot of money. If the employer conduct was intentional, the employer has committed a crime and can expect stiff fines and possible jail time.

Wage laws should be (and usually are) taken seriously by employers. They exist to discourage employee exploitation and to guarantee workers at least a minimal level of compensation. Generally, though, if you feel your rights have been violated, you have to be the one to take the first step. Don't be afraid to contact your local labor department with your questions. Their job is to protect you.

Other Common Question
about Employee Wages

Q: Does my employer have to pay me for vacation time, for holidays, and for sick leave?

A: As the Benefits section of this book explains, your employer doesn't even have to give you vacation time, holidays off, or sick leave (with some exception). Therefore, if the employer does give you these benefits, the employer is still not required by law to pay you for your time off.

Q: I came in late one day so my employer docked me for the time I missed. Is that legal?

A: The law says that you must be paid for the time you actually worked. That means that your employer doesn't necessarily have to pay you for the time you didn't work. If you came in fifteen minutes late, you can be docked for at most fifteen minutes' worth of pay.

Q: I think my wage rights were violated, but that was a few years ago. How much time do I have for filing a claim?

A: The FLSA gives you two years from the time your employer violated the law to formally file a complaint with your state labor department. If your employer intentionally violated the law, you have up to three years.

Q: If I make more than the minimum wage, will I automatically get a raise when the minimum wage goes up?

A: No. Your employer is under no obligation to pay you more when the state or federal government raises the minimum wage. However, if you are making $4.50 an hour and the minimum wage is increased to $4.75, then your employer is obligated to raise your wage to at least $4.75.

15

Employee Hours and Overtime Pay

Jeanie read the memo with disbelief. "Owing to increased foreign competition, we regret that we have no choice but to implement a mandatory overtime policy for all exempt employees beginning next week. Please be as flexible and as understanding as possible in our time of crisis."

Foreign competition? she thought. What a pathetic excuse! The company had been finding new ways to squeeze extra work out of people for years now. More work for the same pay just didn't seem fair.

Everyone's familiar with working overtime. Forty-five-hour weeks, fifty-hour weeks, seventy-hour weeks! Sometimes it seems (and, in fact, the statistics show) that we're working more hours than we have in decades. Surely there must be some law that regulates how much we can be required to work.

Federal Law

The **Fair Labor Standards Act** (FLSA), detailed in the previous chapter, addresses some of these concerns. However, it's important to note that except for a few jobs like truck driver and airline pilot, there's no legal limit on the number of hours your employer can demand of you. Sound oppressive? Feel like you've just been transported back to the 1920s? In the 1990s there is one saving grace: when you work overtime, you may be entitled to overtime pay.

It's common knowledge that overtime pay is equal to one-and-a-half times your regular hourly rate of pay. What's not common knowledge is who's eligible for such a premium. Recall, as chapter 14 noted, that most blue-collar employees are covered by the FLSA (and therefore entitled to overtime pay), whereas most white-collar employees are not. The critical number dividing regular work time from overtime is forty hours work in any given work week. Beyond that, blue-collar employees receive time-and-a-half for each hour worked.

If your hourly rate is consistent each week, say $6.00 per hour, the computation is simple. If you worked fifty hours in a week, ten of those hours were overtime hours. Your employer must compensate you at a rate of $9.00 per hour ($6.00 times one-and-a-half) for each of those ten hours.

For those whose hourly rate varies (for example, those on piece rate or a commission), a "regular rate" of pay is usually calculated as:

$$\frac{\text{all payment for that week minus "exclusions"}}{\text{number of hours actually worked that week}}$$

Therefore, to compute your regular rate, you take your pay for the week, subtract what are called "exclusions" (vacation pay, holiday pay, absence pay, discretionary bonuses, profit sharing, gifts, and employer contributions to your retirement plan and your insurance), and divide the result by the number of hours you worked in the week. That number is used as a basis for overtime pay.

Note that overtime is always calculated on a *weekly* basis. You can put in twelve hours on Monday, ten on Tuesday, and ten on Wednesday and still not receive any overtime pay if your total hours for that week do not exceed forty. In such a situation, your boss can tell you to take the rest of the week off or to work only a few hours on Thursday and Friday so you don't cross the forty-hour threshold. That's all perfectly legal.

However, there is bad news in this area for white-collar employees. In theory, their boss can require them to work twenty-four hours a day, seven days a week, and not pay them a penny more than their stated salary. In addition to white-collar workers (the "professional," "administrative," and "executive" classes defined in chapter 14), some other workers also lack legal entitlement to overtime pay. Among them are:

- most agricultural employees
- air carrier employees
- amusement/recreation establishment employees
- auto, truck, boat, aircraft, and farm implement sales persons
- babysitters
- live-in servants
- cabbies
- some hospital employees
- railroad employees
- news delivery people
- news editors
- TV and radio announcers
- seamen
- forestry/lumber employees
- police and fire department employees

Public Employees

Nearly all state and local government employees are covered by the FLSA. That means the minimum wage and overtime provisions of the Act must be honored by their employers. However, police and fire department employees are specifically exempted from overtime coverage.

One notable difference between public- and private-sector overtime compensation is the use of compensatory ("comp") time in the public sector. Rather than pay state and local government employees time-and-a-half for their overtime, your employers can offer you one-and-a-half hours of unpaid time off for each hour of overtime you work. So if you've worked forty-eight hours one week, your boss can give you twelve hours off (eight overtime hours times one-and-a-half) the next week instead of paying you overtime. This practice can continue in a given year until you've put in 160 hours of overtime (320 in the case of public safety personnel), after which you must be paid in cash for your overtime.

Private-sector employees who are covered by the FLSA cannot be legally denied their overtime pay in favor of comp time. As alluded to earlier, the boss can tell you to stay home for a few days (or a few hours) a week so you won't surpass forty hours.

State Laws

Most states have their own laws regulating hours of work and overtime pay. However, except for California's law which provides for double time when you work more than twelve hours in a day *or* when you work more than eight hours on the seventh day of the work week, and Kentucky's law that requires overtime pay whenever an employee works all seven days of the work week, state laws are generally not more favorable to you than the FLSA. Most, like the federal law, set overtime pay at time-and-a-half for all hours worked beyond forty. In some cases, those who are exempted from the FLSA may be covered under their state law. Your state labor department can provide you with the specific information you need regarding your particular circumstances.

Summary

Returning to the opening scenario, what's Jeanie to do if she doesn't want to work the overtime? What if she has a family, night school, or other obligations? Contrary to what some employers think, most employees do have a life outside of work. Contrary to what many employees think, however, that fact is irrelevant if you're exempted from the FLSA. Exempt employees in Jeanie's firm will just have to bear the mandatory overtime or find a new job.

Nonexempt employees fare a little better under the law because

Q: What does the law say about the hours that minors can work?

A: Regulation of child labor is an important part of the FLSA. The law only restricts the hours of work for those under the age of sixteen. Fourteen- and fifteen-year-olds are permitted to work up to eight hours a day, forty hours a week *when school is not in session* (summertime and school vacations). However, when school is in session, they cannot work more than three hours a day, and no more than eighteen hours a week. Also, fourteen- and fifteen-year-olds can only work between the hours of 7:00 A.M. and 7:00 P.M., except between June 1 and Labor Day when they are permitted to work until 9:00 P.M. Children under fourteen are generally restricted from employment except for farm work with their parents.

Most states have also written their own child labor laws, some that are more stringent than the federal law. In each case, employers must abide by the law that is more restrictive. As with most wage and hour issues, the state labor department is your contact for the specific provisions.

they are entitled to overtime pay. But what if you don't want
work the overtime? What if you have something better to d
Usually, exempt or nonexempt, you're out of luck. The law giv
your employer the right to set your hours. In some cases you g
paid extra, in other cases you don't. But if you don't when t
law says you should, contact your state labor department.

Other Common Questions about Employee Hours and Overtime

Q: Is there any law that entitles me to lunch or coffee breaks?
A: Actually, there are several, but they're state laws and ther
fore only apply to employees in those particular states. Most s;
that employees are to be given at least a thirty-minute break f
every five to eight hours of work. Others include a ten-minu
rest period for every four hours of work. The states that cu
rently have such laws are California, Colorado, Connecticu
Hawaii, Illinois, Kentucky, Maine, Massachusetts, Minnesot
Nebraska, Nevada, New Hampshire, New Mexico, New Yor
North Dakota, Oregon, Pennsylvania, Rhode Island, Was
ington, West Virginia, and Wisconsin. Contact your state lab
department for information on the provisions of your state law

Q: Does my employer have to give me time off to vote?
A: Again, it depends on the state in which you work. Man
states require that employees get between one and three hour
off to vote, often with pay. Some specify that if an employee ha
time either before or after work to vote, the employer does no
need to allow for voting time.

The states that permit you time off to vote include Alaska
Arizona, Arkansas, California, Colorado, Georgia, Hawaii, Illi
nois, Iowa, Kansas, Kentucky, Maryland, Massachusetts, Minne
sota, Missouri, Nebraska, Nevada, New Mexico, New York
Ohio, Oklahoma, South Dakota, Tennessee, Texas, Utah, Washington, West Virginia, Wisconsin, and Wyoming. In almost all of
these states, you'll have to notify your employer in advance of
election day that you'll need time off to vote.

16

Equal Pay for Equal Work

Mike and Kathy are both human resource managers for ABC, Inc. They graduated from the same college and were hired at the same time. Their work load, duties, and hours are identical. So why is Mike's paycheck larger than Kathy's?

E qual pay is one of the most pressing issues for women today. Although the pay statistics often appear to be abused, there is little doubt that pay discrimination continues to be a problem in our society. Both the **Equal Pay Act** (EPA), discussed below, and Title VII, discussed at length in the Discrimination and Discharge section of this book, provide you with the means to challenge any pay discrimination by your employer.

The Equal Pay Act

This is the federal equal pay for equal work law. It requires both public- and private-sector employers to pay the same wages to their male and female employees, provided they are doing work that requires the same skill, effort, and responsibility and is performed under similar working conditions. It is not intended to equalize the pay of, say, a female secretary and a male custodian, even if their work appears to be of the same value to the employer. Rather, it applies to the pay differentials of male and female secretaries and of male and female custodians working for the same employer.

For a change, the Equal Pay Act (EPA) is not complex at all. To evaluate a pay discrimination case under the EPA, a court will simply compare the wages and jobs of a male and female employee who work for the same employer. "Wages" are defined as all the payments made to an employee for his or her services. It includes the employee's base wage or salary, benefits (like vacations, holidays, pensions, and insurance), profit sharing, bonuses, company cars, expense accounts, and any other compensation. If the wages of a male and female employee are different, the next step is to evaluate their respective jobs to see if they require:

1. **equal skill** (similar training, education, experience and abilities),
2. **equal effort** (similar physical and mental energy), and
3. **equal responsibility** (similar importance of their job function, similar accountability for their mistakes, and similar performance of supervisory activities),

and to see if they are performed under:

4. **similar working conditions** (similar physical surroundings and the same risk of injury).

It is important to note that **the two jobs being compared *do not have to be identical,*** only "substantially equal." Moreover, the job titles and job classifications of each employee are irrelevant (for instance, the court won't care if one employee is called a "janitor" while the other is called a "custodial engineer").

If the court finds that the work performed by the employees is relatively equal on the four criteria, but that the wages paid to the male and female employee are different, the lower paid employee (almost always the woman) is in a good position to win the pay discrimination suit.

The Employer's
Defense

But the case doesn't end there. The EPA recognizes that there may indeed be legitimate reasons to pay these two employees differently, even if they are performing the same job. First, many employers pay according to seniority. If a male employee earns more than a female employee in the same job, but the male employee has more seniority, the pay difference may be justified in the eyes of the court.

Second, some employers use merit pay systems that reward high performers with bigger raises. Under this system, as long as the employer regularly evaluates all employees based on their actual performance, pay differences between the sexes may be legal.

A third method of compensation is called incentive pay. Here, employees are paid based on what they actually produce or sell. These "piece-rate" or "commission" pay schemes often result in wage differences for employees in the same job. However, provided that employee performance is fairly and objectively measured, there is probably no violation of the EPA.

Fourth, an employer may be able to prove that some other factors besides sex are responsible for pay disparities between male and female employees. For example, employers may, because of economic conditions, lower the pay rates of all new hires. A new female employee might receive less than a male employee (or another female employee) who was hired just a few days before the new policy went into effect. Other employers may elect to pay "heads of households" more because of their greater needs. A male head of household will therefore earn more than a female who isn't the head of her household, even if both perform the same job. Some courts have found these reasons to be legitimate grounds to pay a man and a woman differently. Others have not. **But the bottom line with all of these employer defenses is: unequal pay for equal work may be legal if it is the result of differences in employee seniority, differences in employee performance, or some other job-related difference that has nothing to do with the employee's sex.**

An Example

Returning to the opening scenario, does Kathy have a case? That will depend on the answers to several questions:

1. Is there a difference in their pay?

Answer: *Yes.*

2. **Do their jobs require equal skill?**

   Answer: *Yes, since they demand similar training, education, experience, and ability.*

3. **Do their jobs require equal effort and responsibility?**

   Answer: *Yes, since their work loads, duties, and supervisory activities are identical.*

4. **Do they have similar working conditions?**

   Answer: *Yes, they both sit in a safe, air conditioned office all day.*

5. **Is there a legitimate reason based on seniority or performance (or maybe something else) that explains their pay differential?**

   Answer: ???

It all comes down to the last question. We know that they have the same seniority but what about performance? If the employer has, for instance, some kind of legitimate merit pay system, and if Mike has outperformed Kathy and received greater raises, Kathy will probably lose her EPA case. If there is no such system or if the employer doesn't evaluate employees fairly and objectively, Kathy could very well win.

And what would she win? Because the EPA is part of the Fair Labor Standards Act, discussed in chapter 14, the remedy for a violation of the EPA is substantially the same as for a violation of the FLSA: double back pay and attorney's fees and costs. Kathy could get back twice what she's owed by ABC, Inc., plus have her legal expenses paid.

Summary

Think about any two employees where you work and ask yourself, "Do these people do essentially the same thing?" Ninety-nine out of one hundred times you'll reach the same conclusion that a court would on the question of equal work. After that, the only issue is whether a legitimate reason can be cited for pay inequities between a male and a female employee doing these jobs. And again, the same things you would think might be legitimate reasons—greater seniority or better performance—are exactly the standards used by the court. A lot equal pay analysis is simple common sense.

Now that you know the law, if you feel that your right to fair pay has been violated, call the U.S. Equal Employment Opportunity Commission.

Other Common Questions about Equal Pay

Q: It seems that both Title VII and the EPA cover sex discrimination in pay. So which should I rely on for my case?

A: It is true that both protect you from pay discrimination on the basis of sex. You can bring both types of suits and each has certain advantages for you. To use Title VII, you must first file a charge with the EEOC. Then you wait until they decide if your case has any merit. If so, they will try to settle it with your employer and, if that doesn't work, they will take your employer to court or issue you a right-to-sue notice that permits you to pursue the case on your own. You cannot simply hire a lawyer and sue your employer under Title VII until you've first let the EEOC investigate the case. That takes time—in some cases a lot of time. If you win, however, under Title VII you may get up to $300,000 plus back pay and legal costs.

If you use the EPA, there is no requirement that you first deal with the EEOC. You can file a lawsuit on your own. Therefore, the advantage of the EPA over Title VII is time. You may get justice much more quickly with the EPA. The trade-off is that if you win, you're only entitled to double what the employer owes you plus legal costs.

So your choice between the two statutes really comes down to this: speed or money. But there's no guarantee of either, no matter which avenue you select.

Q: How much time do I have for filing my EPA case?

A: The EPA gives you up to two years from the time of the last violation of your rights to file. In cases where your employer intentionally (or what they call "willfully") discriminated against you, you have three years.

BENEFITS

17

An Overview
of Benefits Laws

*After a long and frustrating job search, Scott finally landed a job
coordinating parties and bartending for a local caterer. During
the follow-up interview with the owner, he was asked what kind
of salary he would accept. Scott paused, not wanting to sound
too eager, and then responded, "About ten bucks an hour plus
benefits would be fair."*

*"Benefits?!" the owner laughed loudly. "Ten bucks I can do,
but you want benefits? Son, this is the catering business,
not IBM."*

Let's clear up one myth from the very beginning: in general, the
law says that employers do not have to offer you benefits
with your job—no vacation, no holidays, no personal leave, no
severance pay. At present, they do not have to give you life or
health insurance or a pension plan. All that's required by law is
that an employer allow you to take unpaid family and medical
leave, that it pay into your Social Security account, and that it
purchase unemployment and workers' compensation insurance to
protect you. Period. Other benefits are not mandated by the law.

Many employers do provide benefits, though. Some offer them
to attract high-quality employees; others provide them out of a
sense of corporate social responsibility. Although the employer

isn't required to provide benefits, once your employer does provide them, it must comply with several laws.

First of all, a benefit plan cannot discriminate. An employer can't offer vacation time to whites and not to blacks. It can't refuse to give pregnant women or the disabled health coverage when everyone else gets it. It can't demand greater contributions to the pension plan from women simply because they're expected to live longer. **Title VII,** the **Americans with Disabilities Act,** and many similar state laws see to this.

It is also unlawful for a benefit plan to treat older workers adversely. Your employer cannot deny older workers coverage or require that they pay more for coverage. Under current law, a benefit plan must either provide *equal benefits* to employees of all ages, or different benefit packages of *equal cost* to the employer. In an equal benefits plan, everyone gets the same deal regardless of age. In an equal cost plan, your employer sets a maximum dollar amount for the cost of your benefits. Then, after giving you the prices of the various benefits that are available, you choose which benefits you want up to that dollar amount. Neither plan violates the **Age Discrimination in Employment Act.**

With regard to pensions and health insurance, a complex law called the **Employee Retirement Income Security Act** sets boundaries so that promised money and coverage are there when you need them. Also, the **Consolidated Omnibus Budget Reconciliation Act** requires many employers who provide health benefits to permit terminated or laid-off workers to remain on the employer health plan for up to eighteen months at the worker's expense. Both statutes are described in the next chapter.

Time Off

Employers have a lot of latitude in deciding whether you can take time off and whether you'll get paid for it. The only federal laws that address this issue are the **Family and Medical Leave Act,** which grants you up to twelve weeks of *unpaid* leave for childbirth, adoption, or family medical emergencies, and the **Veterans' Reemployment Act** which guarantees time off for those on active or training duty in the armed forces, the reserves, or the national guard. No federal or state laws give you the right to time off with pay.

Part-Time and Temporary Workers

As a growing number of you know, part-timers and temps get shafted when it comes to benefits. That's not because of any law but simply because employers often elect to save money by providing benefits only to their full-time employees. There's nothing illegal about such a policy. However, if an employer gives some part-timers benefits, it must do so for all part-timers. If it gives some temps benefits, it must give all temps benefits.

Summary

This probably hasn't been an encouraging chapter. You'll be even less encouraged to learn that because employers do not have to provide you with many benefits in the first place, they are generally able to take many of them away after giving you adequate notice. But there are exceptions and you do have some rights. The next few chapters detail these rights and advise you on what to do if they are violated.

18

Pension and Health Benefits

Teri had enjoyed a wonderfully fulfilling career as a nurse. The work was so rewarding that her thirty years of dedicated service seemed to pass in the blink of an eye. Nearing retirement, her thoughts turned to sandy beaches, lazy days, and maybe a new convertible. The hospital's generous pension plan would make all this possible.

Six months before she and several of her colleagues became eligible to collect their pensions, the hospital abruptly fired them all and notified them that it had no obligation or intention to grant them retirement benefits.

S ome employers have been known to do unconscionable things, but few acts are more despicable than depriving someone of her pension and her dreams. Fortunately for the millions of people like Teri out there who are counting on that promised pension, the **Employee Retirement Income Security Act** (ERISA) makes such actions illegal.

Federal Law on Retirement Plans

ERISA is the federal law that regulates private-sector, employer-provided pension and health benefit plans. Its primary purpose is to ensure that your retirement money is managed properly so it will be available to you once you've retired. Although it's widely considered the most complicated of all employment laws, the simplified overview of ERISA presented here does address the most pressing concerns in this area. Other, more specific questions you might have can be answered by the U.S. Pension and Welfare Benefits Administration in Washington, DC (202-219-8921).

Conceptually, pension plans are pretty easy to understand. You put in some money, perhaps your employer matches or at least adds to your contributions, and when you reach a certain age, you get that money plus accumulated interest back. Some plans (called **defined benefit** plans) tell you the exact level of retirement benefits you will be receiving, whereas others (called **defined contribution** plans) tell you only what your employer will contribute to your pension. Defined contribution plans are certainly more popular with employers these days since they don't compel them to specify how much they'll pay you in benefits. Instead, under this plan, you and your employer put money in the pot, your employer invests it, and you get whatever is there upon retirement.

Because the employer is handling your money with either type of plan, there's always a potential for abuse. That's where ERISA comes in. The law sets minimum participation requirements, designates when you're legally entitled to what's in your pension fund, makes benefit administrators personally liable for irresponsible fund management, and creates a safety net for pension plans that go bankrupt.

Participation Requirements

To enjoy the tax advantages associated with establishing a pension plan, an employer who provides retirement benefits must permit you to participate in the plan:

1. at age twenty-one or after one year of service (one thousand hours of service in a twelve-month period), or
2. after two years of service provided you immediately become 100 percent "vested" (defined below).

There are only a few exceptions to these requirements:

- If you work for an educational institution, you may have to wait until you reach age twenty-six to participate.

- If you work for a self-employed person, you may have to wait three years to participate.
- If you're an older worker, although you cannot usually be denied participation because of your age, an employer with a defined benefit plan can deny you coverage if you are hired within five years of the plan's normal retirement age.

Vesting Requirements

You always have a legal right to what you've contributed to your pension plan. After all, it's your money. Your employer's contribution is another story. ERISA says that if you don't stick around long enough, your employer can take back all or part of its contribution. If you do stay with your employer, you eventually become "vested," meaning that you are legally entitled to the pension contributions the employer has made on your behalf.

Here's how it works. If you joined your employer's pension plan after 1988, you're entitled to 20 percent of your employer's contribution after three years in the plan, 40 percent after four years, 60 percent after five years, 80 percent after six years, and all of your employer's contribution after seven years of work for that employer. At that point, you're fully vested. If you joined the plan in 1988 or before, the vesting schedule is more gradual, making you wait anywhere from ten to fifteen years before you're fully vested. Check with your benefits administrator to get all the details.

Liability of Administrators

To ensure that those who handle your money do it carefully, ERISA requires your employer to name an administrator of the pension fund, called a "fiduciary." The fiduciary is personally liable for any losses or damage to your pension fund that results from irresponsible investment of that money. That means his or her house, cars, and bank accounts are on the line, so there really is an incentive for fiduciaries to be cautious in their administration of a pension fund.

A Safety Net

What if your company goes out of business and takes the pension plan with it? Or what if the fiduciary ends up in Rio with all your money? ERISA created the Pension Benefit Guarantee Corporation (PBGC) to protect you in such situations. The PBGC is the insurance for your pension. Your employer pays a yearly premium to the PBGC, and in return your pension is guaranteed. It's the same principle as with your bank deposits and the FDIC. If your pension plan disappears, you're covered.

There are two important things to remember about pensions, though. First, **your employer does not have to give you a pension plan.** This is a benefit, and like most benefits, it's not mandated by law. Second, because your employer doesn't have to give you a pension plan, **your employer can terminate any plan that it sets up.** If it does, it must return to you your whole contribution and any employer contribution to which you are legally entitled.

Health Insurance

We're all aware that health insurance reform is on the horizon. In fact, by the time this book is in print, a plan may have already passed Congress. That plan may require your employer to buy you health insurance, or it may not. Under the current law, though, your employer has no such obligation.

In addition to pension plans, ERISA regulates "welfare" plans. Employer-provided welfare plans may offer you benefits in the event of sickness, accidents, hospitalization, disability, death, and other things of this nature. ERISA regulations and protections apply with equal force to any welfare plan your employer provides.

With specific regard to health insurance, in 1985 Congress amended ERISA to permit you to keep your health coverage if you are fired or laid off from your job. The amendment, called the **Consolidated Omnibus Budget Reconciliation Act** (COBRA), applies to all employers (except the federal government) with a health insurance plan and at least twenty employees (smaller employers may be subject to similar state laws—you can call your state insurance commissioner for details).

COBRA says that if you involuntarily lose your job for any

reason except "gross misconduct," you can elect to continue your benefits through your former employer. Gross misconduct typically means you deliberately did something horrible like assaulting your boss or fire-bombing the employer's building. Poor performance, laziness, or excessive absenteeism are not considered gross misconduct.

Former employees and their spouses (including divorced or separated spouses) and dependents are eligible for eighteen months of COBRA coverage. Extended coverage is available to spouses and dependents of employees who die or divorce, and to dependents who become ineligible for the employee's health insurance coverage because they marry or are too old.

The benefits aren't free, of course. You have to pay the premiums. But you do get the employer's group insurance rate rather than a higher individual rate. After eighteen months, your coverage will end unless you elect to stay on and pay the individual rate premium. Coverage could also end during the eighteen months if you fail to make a payment or if you become eligible for another plan or for Medicare.

To elect COBRA coverage, you must notify your former employer within sixty days of your termination.

Summary

This chapter has only provided you with the basics of pension and health benefits law, so don't be discouraged if you don't fully understand ERISA. Many pension lawyers don't fully understand ERISA! What is important for you to remember is that if you have a pension and/or health benefit plan, it must be run in a prudent and nondiscriminatory manner. If you feel your rights are being violated, talk to your benefits administrator. If that proves fruitless, call the U.S. Pension and Welfare Benefits Administration.

Other Common Questions about Pension and Health Benefits

Q: Why does my employer call our pension plan a 401(k)?
A: 401(k) refers to the section of the Internal Revenue Code that permits employers to create plans permitting you to defer part

of your wages until retirement. Employers often match all or part of your contributions and give you a choice about how the pension fund will be invested. However, your employer is not *required* to match anything you put in a 401(k).

Q: Am I entitled to a copy of my employer's pension plan?

A: Absolutely! ERISA requires your employer to provide you with a summary description of the pension plan. If yours has not done so, request one in writing from the personnel department.

Q: What can I expect to receive if I sue my employer for violating my rights under ERISA?

A: Usually people will sue to reclaim benefits that they are due. In the opening scenario, for example, Teri could sue the hospital for her pension benefits. You may recover your legal costs as well, but you are not entitled to punitive damages (additional fines intended to punish your employer).

19

Social Security

By age sixty-three, Bert was pretty sick of the nine-to-five grind. Retirement was an increasingly attractive option. But would he be able to collect Social Security at sixty-three? If so, would it provide enough money for him to retire? And what about health insurance? Leaving the company meant the loss of his medical coverage. Just what kind of life could he expect as a Social Security recipient?

Most people look forward to retirement—a time to sleep late, to vacation at will, to spoil one's grandchildren with attention. For many, though, it's also a time to make do with far less income. Social Security exists to ensure that you have at least some money and health insurance during your retirement years.

Our Social Security system is a huge and complex web of payroll taxes, eligibility requirements, and benefit levels. It would take hundreds of pages to fully explain all of its intricacies. This chapter, therefore, will only provide you with a simple introduction to the system, describing the benefits to which you are entitled and the basic rules of the game. More detailed answers to question about your specific circumstances can be provided free of charge by the U.S. Social Security Administration (800-772-1213).

The Primary Features of Social Security

The Social Security system can be broken down into five parts:

1. **Retirement Security.** Provided that you are eligible for Social Security benefits, you will receive a check each month after you retire. The size of this check depends on the amount of income that you earned over your lifetime.
2. **Survivors' Benefits.** When a worker dies, his or her family may be eligible to receive a monthly check if the family has children under eighteen, if the worker's spouse is at least sixty, if the worker's spouse is at least fifty and disabled, or in a few other narrow instances.
3. **Disability Benefits.** When a worker of any age becomes disabled, he or she may receive money each month from Social Security.
4. **Supplemental Security Income (SSI).** This is a financial assistance program for the very poor who are at least sixty-five, who are blind, or who are afflicted with another disability.
5. **Medicare.** This is the health care component of the Social Security system. It covers the disabled and retirees for both hospital and other medical care.

Eligibility for Social Security Benefits

Almost every employer and employee is required to pay into the Social Security system. To know if you're among them, check your pay stub. If there's a line that says "FICA" with a big deduction next to it, both you and your employer are contributing to the system. Does that mean that you'll be getting anything back? Not necessarily. To be eligible for Social Security benefits, you must have earned enough "credits."

The credit system isn't complicated. You earn one Social Security credit for every $540 in wages you make in a year. You can earn a maximum of four credits per year, so if you've made $2,160 this year, you'll get your four credits. As the law now stands, you must earn forty Social Security credits (which equals ten years of employment) before you're officially eligible for most of the benefits listed above. However, even those without enough credits may still be entitled to SSI money, depending on their income.

Currently, you become eligible for your full retirement benefits at age sixty-five. If you'd prefer to retire earlier, you can still collect Social Security, but as table 19.1 demonstrates, you'll receive only a portion of your full benefit:

TABLE 19.1

Percentage of Benefit for Early Retirees

Retire At	Receive
Age 62	80 percent of your Social Security benefit
Age 63	86⅔ percent of your Social Security benefit
Age 64	93 ⅓ percent of your Social Security benefit

In other words, if your Social Security check would be $500 upon retirement at age sixty-five, you'll only get $400 (80 percent of $500) if you choose to retire at age sixty-two. It's important to note that if you do elect early retirement, your lower monthly benefit remains the same *even after you turn sixty-five*. It's also important to remember that no matter what level of Social Security benefit you receive, it will continue for as long as you live.

A recent change in the law gradually increases the age at which you can collect full retirement benefits. Individuals collecting retirement benefits now are entitled to their full Social Security if they retire at age sixty-five, however, those retiring near the year 2025 will have to wait until they are sixty-seven to collect full benefits. Table 19.2 illustrates when you will be entitled to all of your Social Security benefit.

Even if you will not be entitled to your full retirement benefit until after age sixty-five, you will still be able to retire with reduced benefits at age sixty-two. The reduction, though, is more substantial than for those currently retiring at sixty-two.

Lastly, keep in mind that just as Congress has already changed the law to increase the age when you can collect full benefits, it may attempt to do so again. There are some who say that when the huge baby boomer generation begins drawing benefits, the retirement age may have to be increased to seventy in order for

TABLE 19.2
Full Retirement Benefits

Year of Birth	Age When You Can Receive Full Retirement Benefits
Before 1938	65 years, 0 months
1938	65 years, 2 months
1939	65 years, 4 months
1940	65 years, 6 months
1941	65 years, 8 months
1942	65 years, 10 months
1943–1954	66 years, 0 months
1955	66 years, 2 months
1956	66 years, 4 months
1957	66 years, 6 months
1958	66 years, 8 months
1959	66 years, 10 months
After 1959	67 years, 0 months

the Social Security system to remain solvent. So pay close attention to any developments in this part of the law because they will affect your retirement planning.

How Big Will My Social Security Check Be?

How small is probably the better question. Social Security is intended to replace only a fraction of your preretirement (or predisability) income, so don't count on dining out every night.

Since it's virtually impossible for the average human to calculate his or her benefit, your best bet is to dial 800-772-1213. The Social Security Administration will send you a form to complete that enables them to estimate your benefit for you.

For the truly masochistic, though, here's an outline of the procedure: List your earnings for the past thirty-five years, subtract the earnings that exceeded the maximum subject to Social Security tax for each year, adjust each year's earnings for inflation, add the thirty-five years of earnings, and divide this total by 420 to obtain an average monthly income (called your "Annual Indexed Monthly Earnings"—AIME). Then:

- If your AIME is $339 or less, multiply it by 0.90 to estimate your Social Security benefit.
- If your AIME is between $340 and $2044, use the formula $305.10 + (0.32 \times [AIME - 339])$ to estimate your Social Security benefit.
- If your AIME is greater than $2044, use the formula $850.70 + (0.15 \times [AIME - 2044]$ to estimate your benefit.

If that toll-free number is sounding pretty good right about now, don't be afraid to use it. These are your tax dollars at work.

Disability Benefits

Another important feature of the Social Security system is the benefits it provides to those in society who become disabled outside of work. Your age does not affect your eligibility for these benefits. Rather, the important criterion is your physical or mental condition and the extent to which it prevents you from working.

Disability Insurance (DI) is not intended to cover short-term or partial disabilities. It is reserved for those who have contributed to the Social Security system (or for their families) and who cannot work for at least a year.

Who counts as "disabled?" The law defines a "disability" as the inability to perform gainful work because of a physical or mental impairment that is expected to last at least twelve continuous months or is expected to result in death. If that's not terribly helpful, this may be: there is a series of questions you are asked that should establish whether you are disabled. They are:

1. **Are you working in gainful activity (making $500 or more a month)?** If yes, you get no benefits; if no, go to Question 2.
2. **Does your impairment interfere with your basic work activities?** If no, you get no benefits; if yes, go to Question 3.
3. **Is the impairment so severe that it is on the SSA list of disabilities that automatically will entitle an individual to benefits?** If yes, you receive disability benefits; if no, go to Question 4.

4. **Does the impairment prevent you from performing your usual work?** If no, you get no benefits; if yes, go to Question 5.
5. **Are you capable of performing other work considering your age, experience and education?** If yes, you get no benefits; if no, you receive disability benefits.

You may therefore be granted disability benefits after Questions 3 or 5, depending on the severity of your ailment. If you are entitled to such benefits, there is a five-month waiting period. The level of your benefits, again, depends on your previous income and is computed in the same manner as your retirement benefits, described earlier. DI benefits may also be available to the disabled worker's family if:

1. There are children under eighteen (or in some cases over eighteen but unmarried) in the family, or
2. the spouse of a worker is disabled and over sixty-two, or
3. the disabled spouse of the deceased worker is at least fifty.

Supplemental Security Income (SSI) is also available to the disabled (and to the nondisabled over sixty-four) who have a very low income and few assets. For SSI, you do not need any Social Security credits and there is no waiting period for benefits. It is, in essence, a welfare program that is part of the Social Security system.

Medicare

This is the basic health insurance program within Social Security. It covers people who are at least sixty-five as well as certain disabled people.

There are two major components of Medicare: hospitalization insurance and medical insurance. Hospitalization covers most charges for inpatient hospital care, and a portion of nursing facility, home health care, and hospice bills. Because it is funded out of general FICA revenues, there are no premiums. Most people on Social Security are automatically covered by the hospitalization program.

Most people also qualify for medical insurance at age sixty-five or if they are disabled. For this plan, though, you must pay a small premium. Medical insurance reimburses you for 80 percent of reasonable charges for doctors' services (surgical, diagnostic, X-rays, and so on), outpatient hospital services, and a few others. Not covered are things like prescription drugs, most nursing home care, dental services, eyeglasses, hearing aids, and routine physicals. You can buy this medical insurance at age sixty-five even if you do not qualify for Social Security benefits.

To learn more about eligibility, enrollment, or the specific benefits you'd receive, contact the Social Security Administration and request its *Medicare Handbook*.

Reductions in Your Social Security Check

You may continue to work while collecting retirement benefits; however, this may decrease the level of your benefits. After a certain level of earnings in a year, your Social Security benefit will be reduced in proportion to the wages you earn. As of 1994, if you retire at age sixty-two, sixty-three, or sixty-four, your benefits decrease by one dollar for every two dollars you earn above $8,040. For those retiring between age sixty-five and age sixty-nine, benefits decrease by one dollar for every three dollars earned above $11,160. For those retiring after age sixty-nine, there is no reduction in Social Security benefits no matter how much you earn.

Whether you work or not, your Social Security benefits may be subject to taxes. A single retiree whose total income exceeds $25,000 must pay tax on the Social Security benefits he or she receives ("total income" is defined as non–Social Security income plus one-half of your annual Social Security benefit). For a married couple filing taxes jointly, $32,000 is the magic number. The calculation of the tax is complicated, so pay close attention to the worksheet directions on Form 1040 or consult an accountant. You can also call the Internal Revenue Service toll-free at 800-829-1040 for assistance.

Summary

For every fact about Social Security that this chapter provides, there are probably four or five more not covered. This is why it's important to speak with the experts at SSA, an attorney, or a trained financial planner before making crucial decisions about retirement. Remember, too, that the Social Security system is only intended to prevent the impoverishment of the elderly and the disabled. It won't provide you with a lot of money. So if possible, plan to supplement anything you'd receive from the system with another source of income like a pension plan or an IRA.

Other Common Questions about Social Security

Q: Can I avoid being part of the Social Security system?

A: The answer is almost always no. Just about everyone who works is required to pay Social Security tax and to be part of the system. The only real way out is not to work, and even then you might be covered by your spouse.

Public employees, however, are an exception. Although coverage is not mandatory, many state and local government employers have elected to be part of the Social Security system. If your employer is not among them, you may be covered by a different retirement system. Most federal workers hired after December 31, 1983, are covered by Social Security.

Lastly, there are special rules that apply to military, domestic, farm, nonprofit, church, and family member employees, so if you're working in any of these capacities, check with the SSA for more information.

Q: What if I'm self-employed? I have no employer to pay into the system with me so am I only partially covered?

A: You're still fully covered. However, because there is no employer contribution on your behalf, you must pay twice as much into Social Security. That means that your basic Social Security tax is 15.3 percent of your net earnings up to $60,600 in addition to 2.9 percent of all your net earnings over $60,600. Independent contractors also fall into the category of "self-employed." See your accountant for the details.

Q: If the cost of living goes up, do my Social Security benefits go up as well?

A: Yes. In the early 1970s Congress amended the law to ensure that Social Security benefits keep up with inflation.

20

Family and Medical Leave

After the birth of her child, Tara was basking in the joys of motherhood. Among the first calls she received upon returning from the hospital was one from her boss. "Congratulations!" she said in a very genuine tone. "I hear you're both doing fine. That's terrific! By the way, I'm sorry to break the news so suddenly, but we're absolutely swamped here. I'm going to need you back in a week or so or else I'll have to find a replacement. If you can't, though, I'll understand. I'm a mother too, you know. And I'll see if I can find something else for you as soon as possible."

The purpose of the **Family and Medical Leave Act** (FMLA) is to protect you from having to choose between your family and your job. As a federal law, it sets minimum standards for accommodating the family needs of workers nationwide. Individual states have also drafted laws in this area, and some provide you with greater leave benefits than does the FMLA. This chapter explains the major provisions of these laws.

The FMLA

This recent law gives you the right to take time off from your job for up to twelve weeks in a year for three specific reasons:

- The birth or adoption of a child
- To take care of a seriously ill child, spouse, or parent
- Your own serious personal illness or injury.

Sounds pretty simple, right? Wrong. There are a lot of "but's" and "except's," so be sure to read the next few pages carefully before you decide to disappear from work for three months.

First of all, the FMLA does not grant leave benefits to *all* workers. Although it applies to both public- and private-sector workers, it only covers those whose employers have fifty or more full- and part-time employees. Furthermore, you must have been with your employer for at least twelve months (but they don't have to be consecutive) and at least 1250 hours (I'll save you the math—that's about 156 eight-hour work days) before you can take advantage of the FMLA. All told, it's been estimated that this law actually covers about 40 percent of American workers.

A second important point is that your employer does not have to pay you for the days you are on leave. The company can require you, or you may request, to use any paid leave you might have first (personal days, vacation, sick leave, and so on) and then take whatever is left of your twelve weeks in unpaid leave. If you receive health benefits from your employer, the law requires that those benefits be maintained while you are on leave.

Reasons for Leave

When can you take family or medical leave? Mothers' and fathers' leave can begin upon the birth or adoption of a child and can continue for up to twelve weeks. You can also take leave to care for a spouse, child, or parent who has a "serious health condition," that is, a condition that requires inpatient care at a hospital, residential care facility, or hospice, or as a condition that requires continuing treatment by a doctor. So if your spouse is in the hospital, or your parent in a nursing home has a heart condition, you can request leave to attend to him or her for a few days. If a family member's back problems require him to see a doctor regularly for check-ups and therapy, you can accompany him there.

The definition also covers situations where someone is not "seriously" ill, but cannot care for his or her own hygienic or nutritional needs. If, for example, your five-year-old child gets sick while at school, you are permitted to take family leave for the balance of the work day to go home and care for him. This type of leave, called "intermittent leave," allows you to take a few hours here and there as necessary.

Furthermore, the FMLA provides for what is called "reduced schedule leave" for those who need to care for a family member with a serious health condition, say, every afternoon, every Friday morning, or on some other regular basis. Your employer must accommodate your request for this leave, but it may also temporarily transfer you to a job with equivalent pay and benefits if you require reduced schedule leave. This transfer provision of the FMLA is intended to help employers avoid any serious work disruptions that may result from your new schedule. Remember, though, whether you take leave all at once, or on an intermittent basis, or in the form of a reduced schedule, your employer does not have to provide you with more than twelve work weeks of leave in any given twelve-month period.

The FMLA is a little more rigid if you are the one who is ill or who needs to visit a doctor regularly. The law says that you can take leave for (1) a health condition that prevents you from performing your job functions and requires more than just a few days off, or (2) continued monitoring of your condition by a physician (for example, routine exams after a heart attack). In other words, a headache at noontime does not entitle you to leave. Neither would a common cold allow you to stay home. Because it is not the intent of the law to substitute for (or to create) a sick leave policy in your company, only serious problems like appendicitis, severe respiratory conditions, emphysema, heart or back surgery, severe morning sickness, and ongoing complications from pregnancy enable you to take leave. So although you may use family leave because a young child is ill, you may not do so for your own minor illness.

Can I Be Fired or Demoted for Taking Leave?

As long as you meet all of the eligibility requirements of the FMLA, your employer cannot punish you in any way for exercising your legal right to take family or medical leave. If, for example, Tara in the opening scenario had been with the company for at least 1250 hours over the past twelve months, and her company employed at least fifty people, her boss *must* permit her to take up to twelve weeks of unpaid leave, *must* continue her health benefits (if the company offers them), and *must* allow her to return to her old position (or an equivalent position that has the same pay, benefits, and working conditions) at the end of her leave. The only exception to this rule is if Tara is one of the highest paid employees (top 10 percent) in the company. Otherwise, her boss is violating the law in this telephone conversation.

State Laws

If the FMLA doesn't cover you, or if its leave provisions do not meet your needs, you may still look to a state law for protection. Most states have family and medical leave laws. Some have provisions that are identical to or lesser than those of the FMLA. Others are more generous, guaranteeing greater leave benefits and/or covering employees who fall through the cracks in the FMLA. If your state law is different from the FMLA, you can rely on the one that provides you with the most benefits.

Listed below are the state leave laws whose provisions are broader or more liberal than the provisions of the FMLA. For more detailed information about your state law, you can call your state's labor department.

Alaska   State and local government employees whose employers have at least twenty-one workers and who have worked at least thirty-five hours a week for six consecutive months or 17.5 hours a week for twelve consecutive months are covered. They can take up to eighteen weeks of leave in any twelve-month period for the birth or adoption of a child.

California   Maximum leave is four months over a twenty-four-month period for those with at least one year of service and whose employers have at least fifty workers. All employers must allow time off for school conferences about suspended children. Employers of twenty-five or more employees must allow up to four hours leave per year per child for school visits.

Colorado   State employees' maximum leave is three months per twelve-month period once they have at least one year of service.

Connecticut Private-sector employees who have worked at least one thousand hours in one year are eligible for leave provided that their employer has at least seventy-five workers. All state employees are eligible for leave after six months of employment.

District of Columbia Employers of twenty or more must provide leave to those who have served at least one thousand hours over the course of one year. Leave can be taken for birth, adoption, and to care for ill family members, which includes "domestic partners" of at least one year.

Florida Law covers all state government employees and sets the maximum leave at six months.

Georgia Leave can be taken by state government employees for up to twelve weeks in any twelve-month period for birth, adoption, or illness of a child, parent, spouse, or spouse's parent.

Hawaii Those whose employers have more than one hundred workers are eligible for four weeks of leave after six months of service.

Illinois Law covers state government employees and sets the maximum leave at one year for family responsibilities. Employers of fifty or more workers must grant up to eight hours per school year for an employee to attend school activities that cannot be scheduled during the employee's nonwork hours.

Kansas Law covers state government workers and sets the maximum leave at one year. Probationary state employees get up to sixty days of leave.

Louisiana All employers must give forty hours of paid leave to those who work twenty or more hours per week and donate bone marrow.

Maine Private and local government employees with one year of service whose employers have at least twenty-five workers and all state government employees are eligible for ten weeks of leave over the course of any twenty-four-month period.

Massachusetts After three months of employment, full-time female employees in the private sector whose employers have at least six workers and all full-time female public employees are eligible for eight weeks of leave for birth or adoption.

Minnesota All those with at least one year of half-time service are eligible for six weeks of leave if their employer has at least twenty-one employees. Employees must be allowed to use paid sick leave for child's illness and are permitted up to six hours of leave per school year for activities that cannot be scheduled during the employee's nonwork hours. Also, all employers must provide forty hours of paid leave to those who work at least twenty hours per week and who donate bone marrow.

New Jersey Those who work for employers of fifty or more employees and who have worked at least one thousand hours in one year are eligible for twelve weeks of leave over the course of any twenty-four-month period.

North Dakota Law covers state employees who have one year of service of at least twenty hours per week. It sets the maximum leave at sixteen weeks over the course of any twelve-month period.

Oklahoma Law covers state government employees who have at least six months of service. It sets the maximum leave at twelve weeks over the course of any twelve-month period.

Oregon Those whose employers have at least twenty-five employees and who have at least ninety days of service are eligible for birth/adoption leave of twelve weeks over the course of any twelve-month period. Those whose employers have at least fifty employees and who have at least one hundred and eighty days of service of twenty-five or more hours per week are eligible for medical leave of twelve weeks over the course of any twelve-month period. All employers must provide forty hours of paid leave to those who work at least twenty hours per week and who donate bone marrow.

Rhode Island Private-sector employees whose employers have at least fifty employees, local government employees whose employers have at least thirty employees, and all state employees are eligible for thirteen weeks of leave over the course of any twenty-four-month period provided that the employee has worked one year or more for at least thirty hours per week.

Tennessee   Females who work for employers of one hundred or more are eligible for four months of maternity leave once they have one year of service. Female public employees are also eligible for thirty days leave for adoption.

Vermont   Those who work for employers of ten or more are eligible for parental leave of twelve weeks over the course of any twelve-month period once they've worked thirty hours per week for one year. "Parental leave" provides time off for the illness of the employee's parents or the spouse's parents. Those who work for employers of fifteen or more employees are eligible for other family and medical leave (birth, adoption, ill child, spouse or employee) under the same terms.

Wisconsin   Those who work for employers of fifty or more are eligible for up to six weeks for birth or adoption, and two weeks for illness once they've worked at least one thousand hours in a one-year period.

Summary

The intent of the Family and Medical Leave Act is to allow individuals to attend to family needs without jeopardizing their jobs and careers. Many employers, however, have long recognized the unfairness of asking employees to sacrifice either job or family and have therefore developed leave policies of their own, some that are very generous. Ask about your employer's policy first. Check your employee handbook. You may be surprised by what you find. If your employer does not permit family and medical leave, though, keep in mind that you may still be entitled to temporary time off by law.

Other Common Questions about Family and Medical Leave

Q: Can men take leave for the birth or adoption of a child?
A: Absolutely. The FMLA applies to both men and women equally.

Q: Do I have to notify my employer that I'll be taking leave?

A: If the leave is foreseeable, as in the case of birth or adoption, you must give your employer thirty days notice. Otherwise, you can generally take leave immediately.

Q: Can my employer require that I provide a doctor's note to prove that I needed to take leave?

A: The employer can require certification for "serious health conditions" but not for birth or adoption. The employer is also permitted to get a second opinion at its own expense. If the two opinions differ, a third opinion, offered by someone agreed upon by you and your employer, will break the tie and be final.

Q: What if I don't want to return to my job after taking leave? Is there any penalty?

A: Your employer can't force you to come back if you don't want to. However, if your employer has provided you with benefits during your leave and you do not return to work, the FMLA says that your employer can charge you for the benefit premiums it paid during your leave period.

Q: At my worksite, there are only forty-five employees. Does that mean I can't take advantage of the FMLA?

A: Not necessarily. First, you may be covered by a state law that requires smaller employers to provide leave. Check with the "State Laws" section of this chapter or your state labor department to determine if this is the case.

Second, the FMLA says that you are covered if your employer has fifty or more employees at your worksite or *within a seventy-five-mile radius of your worksite*. This means that if, for example, you work in a bank that has only twenty employees at your branch you are still covered by the FMLA as long as that bank employs at least thirty other people in all of its branches within seventy-five miles of your office.

Q: Where do I go to report violations of the FMLA?

A: Contact the Wage and Hour Division of the U.S. Department of Labor. If you think that your state family and medical leave law has been violated, contact your state labor department.

21

Unemployment Benefits

The boss in the butcher shop, a man with absolutely no managerial skills whatsoever, would constantly subject his employees to verbal abuse. Finally, when she could no longer take it, Maria, a long-time employee, picked up a whole roast beef and threw it at him, hitting him squarely in the head. Not surprisingly, she was immediately fired.

Now, with no income, Maria filed for unemployment benefits. Still smarting from the embarrassment of the roast beef incident, her ex-boss has decided to challenge her application.

Back in the 1930s, when the Great Depression deprived many people of their jobs, we created an unemployment system. The first goal of this system was to prevent jobless workers from slipping into poverty. The second was to get the economy growing. When many people have little or no money to spend, the economy shrinks, making it even less likely that people will find jobs.

The federal government established the general guidelines of the unemployment system and supported it with employer taxes. The state governments determined the specific eligibility requirements and set the benefit levels for those who became unemployed in their jurisdictions. Today, every state has an unemployment system.

Now what about Maria? Is she eligible for benefits? If so, for how long? And how much will she receive? This chapter provides you with the answers to these and other questions about what to expect from the unemployment system in your state.

Who Can Collect
Unemployment Benefits?

Just about everyone—part or full time, public or private sector, blue or white collar—is covered by unemployment insurance. The few exceptions are agricultural workers, independent contractors, and the self-employed. All other workers may be eligible for benefits if they lose their jobs.

But you don't automatically get unemployment benefits because you're not working. There are some ground rules. First, you must have lost a job that you held for at least three months. In essence, you have to earn your way into the system by working a bit. Second, you must have lost that job for some reason that wasn't really your fault. This means that people who voluntarily quit their jobs are almost never able to collect unemployment. Whether you're going to move, or you want some time off, or you're pregnant, or you're simply bored with your job and want to look for something else, if you leave for personal reasons like these, you get no benefits.

The law recognizes, though, that some people quit because of an intolerable situation at work. For instance, if you're subject to harassment, quitting your job may be justified. Or if the secondhand smoke in your office is unbearable and your employer won't do anything about it, quitting may be your only alternative. **The rule is: workers who voluntarily leave their jobs are not eligible for unemployment benefits, but those who are forced to quit by someone or something may be eligible.** In other words, it's not quite as simple as "You quit, so no benefits." It's really "You quit, so you get no benefits unless you have a very legitimate reason."

Laid-off workers, by contrast, can almost always collect unemployment checks. The system was designed to help them out until they are recalled to their job or find other employment.

If you've been fired, though, you're in a gray area. Many people who are fired get unemployment benefits, but some don't. The criterion for entitlement, again, is the loss of your job for a reason that wasn't really your fault.

So you're incompetent, or you had an accident at work. You were absent a few too many times, you had a personality clash with your boss, or you botched a project and cost the firm a couple of million dollars. You didn't do it on purpose. You didn't intend to break any rules or harm your employer's business. As most state laws are written, these things are *not your fault,* and therefore will not prevent you from collecting unemployment benefits.

But what if you threw a roast beef at your boss? Is *that* "your fault?" As a general rule, people who are fired for "misconduct" are not entitled to unemployment benefits. Such individuals are considered to have lost their jobs for something that was indeed their fault. The big question is what constitutes "misconduct?" Her pink slip says that Maria was insubordinate when she flung that beef. It doesn't use the word "misconduct." How does the unemployment agency decide what's misconduct and what isn't? And do they even consider the fact that Maria had a good reason for her actions, and probably should have nailed her boss with a chunk of limburger as well?

Agencies take a very commonsensical approach to this issue. They look at all the facts of the case and decide whether the terminated employee deliberately did something improper. If so, it's usually ruled misconduct. Things like sleeping on the job, stealing from the company, or intentionally slacking off or violating a work rule are clearly misconduct under this standard. You did it on purpose and there's no question that it's your fault.

Swearing at your boss could be misconduct as well. However, if the action was provoked, the unemployment judge would take that fact into account. If your boss slapped you on the bottom and you responded with a few choice words not found in Webster's, the judge probably wouldn't call that misconduct. In the case of Maria, the fact that her boss continually abused her would be relevant information. She was provoked and maybe she just snapped. It's conceivable that her actions won't be considered misconduct, but, rather, justifiable retaliation. If so, she won't get her job back, but she will get unemployment benefits.

The Process for Collecting Benefits

Claiming your unemployment benefits can be a very easy thing
to do sometimes. For your first claim after you've lost your job,
go to your local unemployment office with the following: your
Social Security card, your driver's license or other forms of ID,
and the names and addresses of past employers. The agency will
contact your last boss or a person in the human resources department of your former employer for his or her version of why
you are no longer employed. Based on the information that you
and your employer supply, the agency will make an initial determination about your eligibility for benefits. If it's clear that you
were laid off or fired for something other than misconduct, you
will begin receiving weekly benefits.

But the process can get considerably more complex. After its
initial determination, the agency gives both you and your employer about two weeks to appeal the decision. If you are *denied*
benefits, you're entitled to a hearing during which a judge will
try to sort out questions about your eligibility (for example, Did
you quit? Was it for a good reason? Were you fired for misconduct?). Usually you'll need an attorney who's familiar with your
state's unemployment system to successfully navigate this stage
of the process.

If the initial agency decision says that you *are* eligible for benefits, your employer can appeal to try to deny you those benefits.
Why would an employer challenge your entitlement to an unemployment check? Because the more people an employer has collecting unemployment, the higher the employer's unemployment
tax will be. The system is designed that way so employers have a
disincentive to fire you or to lay you off. Once you're unemployed, though, an employer might want to prevent you from
drawing benefits so its tax doesn't increase. If your former
employer appeals, just like if you appeal, there will be a hearing
in front of an unemployment compensation judge to resolve the
dispute.

And if either party doesn't like the result, the judge's decision
can also be appealed to your state's unemployment review
board, and then to the state courts. A very small percentage of
claims go this far, though, so don't worry about this possibility.

Typically, the process is straightforward and reasonably pain-less. Your state unemployment agency can answer any questions you have about your specific circumstances.

Unemployment Benefit Levels

One question everyone asks is, "How much do I get?" Once you've applied and it's established that you are eligible for bene-fits, you'll get a weekly check, usually after a one-week waiting period. Ten states have no waiting period (Alabama, Connecti-cut, Delaware, Iowa, Kentucky, Maryland, Michigan, Nevada, New Hampshire, and Wisconsin), and four others pay you retro-actively for your waiting period after a few weeks on unemploy-ment (Missouri, Minnesota, New Jersey, and Texas).

In most states the amount of your check will be approximately one-half of your average weekly salary or one-half of the state-wide average weekly salary, whichever is less. At most, you'll receive benefits for twenty-six weeks (thirty in Massachusetts), but some states are willing to extend your benefits after the twenty-six-week period if the unemployment rate is very high. As you've probably seen on the news, the federal government has also come through with money on several occasions to extend unemployment benefits beyond twenty-six weeks.

And speaking of the federal government, it's going to expect its share of your unemployment check come April 15. Usually, the taxes aren't deducted from your check up front as they are on your paycheck, so plan ahead.

Losing Your Benefits

In addition to starting at a new job, there are several things that will disqualify you from continuing to receive unemployment compensation. First, your state requires that you look for work while on unemployment. This often means that you have to sup-ply the unemployment agency with your weekly employment contacts to keep your benefits coming. If you don't, you may be disqualified from receiving any more money.

Second, you'll be required to accept suitable employment when it becomes available. What is "suitable" depends on your usual occupation and pay level, and your education, work experience, skills, age, and disabilities. A teacher, for instance, doesn't have to take a job as a file clerk, and an executive doesn't have to accept something in middle management. "Suitable" usually means a job at the same level as what you were doing before. If you *do* neglect to take a suitable job when it's offered, you're risking disqualification for unemployment benefits.

Third, your benefits may also cease if you become a full-time student or if you begin to collect other income like severance pay or workers' compensation. In most states, if you elect to take part-time employment while searching for a full-time job, you may continue to receive benefits, but they'll be reduced proportional to what you earn at work. Temporary full-time employment will usually suspend your unemployment benefits until the temp job has ended.

Unemployment Due to Business Closings

As mentioned earlier, the unemployment system protects you if you are laid off. There's also a law that specifically addresses layoffs, the **Worker Adjustment and Retraining Notification Act.** This federal law says that any employer who has at least one hundred employees must notify employees sixty days in advance of a business closing or of a layoff that involves more than fifty employees. If your employer is going to close, with few exceptions, you're entitled to two months' notice. This feature of the law explains why it has such a strange name: its backers wanted a catchy acronym: WARN.

But Congress was apparently more concerned about creating a catchy acronym than with protecting your rights because, as well intentioned as the law may seem, *it levies no penalties against noncomplying employers and no agency is responsible for enforcing it.* You can't just call the U.S. Department of Labor on this one. There's no free advice. And there's no stiff penalty if your employer ignores the law. You and your coworkers have to sue your employer in federal court. If you win, you could be awarded up to three years in back pay and benefits. But in many cases, an employer who has just closed down probably isn't rolling in dough. A victory might simply entitle you to a place in line with all of the other creditors (and it won't be at the head of the line!).

In addition to WARN, a handful of states have business closing laws of their own (Connecticut, Hawaii, Kansas, Maine, Maryland, Massachusetts, Michigan, Minnesota, Montana, New Jersey, New York, Oregon, South Carolina, Tennessee, and Wisconsin). The provisions in most of them are similar to those in WARN, but occasionally apply to smaller employers and/or require employers to give you a little more notice. However, few of these laws have any teeth either. To inquire about the guidelines in your state, you can call your state labor department

Summary

The unemployment system is a safety net that protects those who involuntarily lose their jobs. If you are laid off or fired, you should contact your local unemployment office right away for specific instructions on what to do. In most cases, you'll be eligible to collect an unemployment check.

But if you voluntarily quit for personal reasons or are fired for deliberate misconduct, you're seldom going to be entitled to any benefits. However, it's still a good idea to speak with a representative from the unemployment agency about your eligibility, just to be sure. And when in doubt, file a claim.

Other Common Questions about Unemployment Benefits

Q: If I voluntarily retire, can I collect unemployment benefits until Social Security kicks in?

A: Not if you voluntarily retire. If you're forced to retire, then you're probably eligible. In that case, though, you might also be able to win an age discrimination suit (see chapter 4).

Q: Can I collect unemployment benefits when I go on strike?

A: In almost all cases, if you are on strike, you get no unemployment benefits. In some states, however, you will get some benefits if your employer is able to continue operations during the strike.

Also, if your employer locks you out of the plant, or if your employer permanently replaces you, you'll often be eligible to collect unemployment benefits.

Q: My employer didn't inform us that the company was going out of business. How much time do my coworkers and I have to sue the company?

A: Another dirty little secret of the Worker Adjustment and Retraining Notification Act is that it sets no time limit for suing your employer. So employees don't know what the rules are and courts have to make them up as they receive cases.

The few courts that have addressed this question haven't even reached the same conclusion. Currently, you have only six months to sue if you live in New York or Texas, but you have six years if you live in Michigan. Because of this inconsistency, the best advice is to get an attorney quickly and to be sure your suit is filed within six months of the plant closing.

EMPLOYEE
SAFETY
AND
HEALTH

22

Your Right to a
Safe Workplace

Ken was an ironworker who tragically fell two hundred feet to his death while on the job. The tragedy was only compounded by the fact that every few years, after the government inspection, the construction company would be fined for failing to install a safety net that would have saved Ken's life. Because the fines were never more than $1000, though, the company found it cheaper to pay them than to comply with the law.

Lots of people get injured at work, many become sick, and some even die. Every year in the United States over six million workers sustain some type of injury or illness from their jobs. According to a recent government study, in the 1980s, an average of seventeen people died at work everyday. But, equally regrettable, there isn't much out there to encourage employers to improve these statistics.

Congress and the states have responded to this situation with laws that seek to achieve two goals. The first goal is *prevention* of workplace injuries. The **Occupational Safety and Health Act,** administered by the Occupational Safety and Health Administration (OSHA), is the centerpiece of federal efforts to minimize the risk you'll be exposed to at work. Its attempts to regulate workplace hazards are detailed in this chapter.

The second goal is *compensation* of workers who have been harmed through the performance of their jobs. Your state has a workers' compensation system in place that provides partial replacement of your income and coverage of your medical bills if you get hurt at work. Chapter 23 describes the specifics of these systems.

The Federal Law

The Occupational Safety and Health Act is a federal statute that applies to almost all private-sector employers. The Act says that **your employer has a general duty to provide you with a working environment that is free from recognized hazards that may cause serious harm or death.**

"Recognized hazards" are those dangers that are common to your particular line of work. For example, in the construction industry, one recognized hazard is the possibility of falling from a beam twenty stories in the air. In a chemical factory, several toxic fumes would be considered recognized hazards.

In addition to its general duty, your employer must comply with specific OSHA standards for your industry. The secretary of labor, the official who oversees OSHA, determines things like:

- How loud your plant can be
- How warm or cold it can be
- How much of a particular substance you can be exposed to at work
- Ventilation standards
- Lighting standards
- How clean your workplace must be
- The number of emergency exists, fire alarms, and fire extinguishers that must be present
- How toxic substances should be handled and stored
- The amount of employer-provided training necessary for employees who handle toxic substances.
- The protective equipment required for your face, hands, feet, and respiratory system
- The suitability of your drinking water at work, the cleanliness of your restrooms, and even the number of toilets per employee.

In all, there are over 3,600 standards that employers must obey. The sheer number of these regulations is one reason that OSHA standards are often neglected or ignored by employers.

Problems with enforcing the law are another reason. OSHA is responsible for inspecting your worksite to ensure that your employer is meeting its safety and health standards. However, the agency has only about three thousand inspectors. That may sound like a lot, but consider this: there are more than five million workplaces in the United States. When you do the math, any given workplace can expect an OSHA inspection approximately every seventy or eighty years!

Some industries, however, are inspected more than others. OSHA tends to focus its limited resources on those industries that are particularly dangerous or that involve the greatest risks. Also, twenty-three states have agencies similar to OSHA that perform inspections and pick up some of the slack in enforcing the law (see table 22.1). Depending on where you live and work, then, you may indeed witness some type of government safety inspection during your lifetime.

In addition to random inspections, OSHA and its state counterparts respond to employee complaints and employee requests for inspections. Let's say you work at a chemical plant—or even in an office—and you're regularly breathing in something that nauseates you. Your boss refuses to do anything about it. You can take your complaint to OSHA and request that it investigate the situation.

TABLE 22.1
States with Safety and Health Agencies

Alaska	Maryland	South Carolina
Arizona	Michigan	Tennessee
California	Minnesota	Utah
Connecticut*	Nevada	Vermont
Hawaii	New Mexico	Virginia
Indiana	New York*	Washington
Iowa	North Carolina	Wyoming
Kentucky	Oregon	

*The Connecticut and New York agencies apply to state and local government employees only.

Your request must be in writing, must state the reason for your complaint, and must be signed. If you'd like, OSHA will keep your identity confidential (beware, though—in many cases the boss will know who filed the complaint because you probably already complained to him or her). OSHA will then investigate the conditions and if it finds a violation of the standards or of your employer's general duty, it will fine your employer and order that the problem be fixed.

Fines generally range from $1 to $7,000 for a single violation that's not too serious, and up to $70,000 for serious or repeat violations. Often, however, that's chicken feed to an employer, especially when fixing the problem could mean millions of dollars. This is another reason that many people think that occupational safety and health law needs to be reformed if it's truly going to protect you.

Refusing to Do a Job

Let's say you conclude that a certain task you've been assigned is dangerous or hazardous. You might tell your boss that you'd rather not risk it. If your boss assures you that there's no danger or tells you in no uncertain terms to get back to work, can you refuse to perform the dangerous task? If you do refuse, can you be disciplined or even fired?

The answers to these questions aren't perfectly clear yet, but generally, **if you reasonably believe that a dangerous task will cause you physical injury or illness, and if indeed there is some violation of OSHA standards involved, you cannot be disciplined or fired for refusing to perform the task.**

A few details . . . The risk involved can be immediate (like falling several feet) or long term (breathing in a carcinogen). You are protected in both cases. Also, whatever the perceived danger, you must ask your employer to correct the problem first. If your employer refuses, then you may be able to refuse as well. If you do get fired, contact OSHA or your state agency right away. You might face a long and tough battle to regain your job, but at least you'll have an ally to handle your case.

Your Right to Know about Workplace Hazards

Do you know what hazardous substances exist in your workplace? In most states, your employer must provide you with this information. These "right to know" laws require almost all employers in the state to inform their employees of toxic and dangerous substances that are on the premises. In factories, the list may be several pages long; in banks, it may simply cover a few cleaning products in a janitor's closet. Employers must also clearly label the substances and, in many cases, provide training on protective measures, hazard identification, and emergency response for employees who may be exposed to the substances.

Medical Records

As chapter 13 indicated, you may have a right to access some of your personnel records. Under OSHA, your employer must keep your medical records for thirty years after you leave the company, and must maintain records of your exposure to hazardous substances. *All employees,* regardless of what state they live in, have the right to access their medical and exposure records upon request.

Summary

You don't have to be working in a meat-packing company to be protected by occupational safety and health laws. However, as this chapter has implied, because of weak monitoring and enforcement, the protection you do receive isn't substantial. While on paper you do have the right to a safe and healthful workplace, your employer may find it cheaper to violate this right than to comply with the law.

Additionally, it could take quite a long time to seek recourse through OSHA or your state safety and health agency. That doesn't mean you shouldn't pursue your case with the help of the government. **By all means, explore every avenue available to you.** Just be prepared for delays.

There is one thing you can do to reduce the number of safety problems at work, though: speak with your boss about creating an employee safety committee. Many firms, both union and nonunion, have them. In cooperation with the supervisors and managers, these committees monitor safety and health issues at work, nip little safety problems in the bud, and develop policies to prevent workplace injury and illness. And, just as important, they provide some sort of grievance procedure for your complaints. This way you can get your problem solved quickly without dealing with government bureaucracy.

Ask your boss about it. Generally, both employers and employees consider safety committees to be a good alternative to relying solely on OSHA.

23

Workers' Compensation

Lisa had been promoted. No longer was she just another face in the gauntlet of perfume ladies at Macy's Department Store. Now, as a beauty consultant, she worked behind the cosmetics counter. Customers were now coming to her and the commissions she received had doubled.

Her prospects were bright until she knelt down to retrieve some coins that had fallen out of the cash register. As she stood back up, she smacked the back of her head on the open register drawer, leaving her with a concussion, some large medical bills, and several weeks of no income.

Workers' compensation insurance is available to almost every worker, full-time or part-time, public or private sector, blue or white collar. Your employer buys it to protect you in case you suffer some kind of serious injury on the job. Whether you're injured by a forklift, a stack of crates, or a cash register, "workers' comp," as it's called, covers you. Even those who appear to have the cushiest of jobs are protected. For instance, lawyers who strain themselves lifting briefcases or reaching for a book have collected *thousands* of dollars for their work-related injuries!

A brief history: before there were workers' comp laws, injured employees would have to sue their employers in court, and, because courts made it almost impossible for employees to win, there was little chance that employees would be compensated for their injuries. But over time employers got tired of being sued and workers demanded a more sympathetic system. States responded by writing workers' comp laws, and now every state has one.

That means that there are fifty variations of how the law works. But there are plenty of commonalities. This chapter will describe the most important features of your workers' comp system, and will explain when you will be entitled to benefits and how to get them.

What is Workers' Compensation?

If you don't know for sure, you're not alone. Many people have heard the term or know of workers' comp, but have no idea how it works or if it applies to them.

Your employer is required by the state to purchase workers' comp insurance. It's just like most other insurance policies. If you get hurt at work, your employer's workers' comp policy covers your medical expenses and replaces part of your income. As a result, just like other insurance policies, your employer's premium will then rise. To keep costs down, therefore, employers have an incentive to (1) minimize accidents on the job, and (2) challenge any workers' comp claims that they think are bogus.

For the most part, your workers' comp system is the only avenue you have to collect if you're injured at work. Only if you have a case for claiming that your employer *intended* to injure you can you sue your employer in court. The workers' comp system is designed to be your only remedy for injury claims, but is also designed to be a lot faster than any justice you'd receive through a court. So in essence, both parties win. You get quick compensation and no medical bills; your employer avoids expensive lawsuits.

But if you and your employer disagree about whether you're entitled to workers' comp, and you can't go to court, where do you go? Each state has a workers' compensation agency that administers the law and resolves disputes. It's a separate court system for workers' comp claims. If you get hurt, the laws say you must notify your employer "promptly" (translation: usually within a week) and file a claim with the workers' comp agency. The time limit for filing with the agency ranges from ninety days to six years, depending on where you live, but in most states it's either one or two years. Many people file right away after an accident to get benefits as quickly as possible. The phone number of your state agency can be found in Appendix A.

Once you've filed, your employer can agree to pay your claim or can challenge it with the workers' compensation agency. A challenge means that your employer thinks you were not actually injured or that your injury was not suffered in the workplace. If your claim is challenged, the workers' compensation agency will schedule a hearing data for your case. The agency will probably try to settle the case informally first, but if that doesn't work, you'll find yourself in front of a workers' comp judge explaining what happened and offering any evidence you have.

Employers have evidence too. They can provide their own witnesses, doctor's reports, and sometimes even videotape to prove that you don't have the injury that you are claiming. Because of workers' comp fraud (workers taking advantage of the system), it's becoming more and more common for employers to hire private detectives to film the off-duty activities of employees who file a claim. Legal? For the most part, yes! As long as you're outside your house or in some public place, your activities aren't considered private. The courts usually allow videotaping that doesn't involve "private" activities.

The moral of the story? Don't file false claims. Workers' comp insurance is expensive and employers don't want it to go any higher. If you're faking an injury, there's a good chance you'll get caught. Then you can kiss both your claim and your job good-bye.

But if you do have a legitimate claim and you happen to lose your case before the workers' comp judge, you can appeal the decision to a higher review board, and ultimately to the state appeals and supreme courts. For the appeal, you won't have to give testimony all over again. The board or court will simply read the record of your hearing and render a decision (states do vary in the exact procedure they follow, though).

What Type of Injuries Are Covered by Workers' Compensation?

The assembly line gave you a hangnail or you received a paper cut while refilling the copy machine. Workers' comp is not intended for such calamities. But what about a jammed thumb or a bruised knee? What if I break my toe? Does someone really have to be run over by a forklift or receive a head injury to collect workers' comp?

No. However, regardless of where you live and work, your claim must pass four tests for you to collect benefits. You must sustain (1) a personal injury (2) from an accident (3) that arises out of employment (4) during the course of employment.

"A Personal Injury"

Most physical injuries (like breaking your leg) as well as occupational diseases, other illness, and death are all considered personal injuries. Less clear are cases involving a mental or psychological injury (like workplace stress or a nervous breakdown from your boss cracking the whip too hard). Some states say that these conditions pass the personal injury test whereas others do not.

"From an Accident"

An accident can be a sudden occurrence (like a box falling on you), but it doesn't have to be. It can also be something that happens to you over time. For instance, a group of mechanics may get pneumonia because their employer forced them to work on cars during the coldest two days of the winter despite the fact that the garage's heating system kept breaking down.

An accident will, however, usually have to be both unexpected and traceable to a definite time, place, and cause. The pneumonia could meet these requirements if the mechanics didn't have any symptoms before the two days of working in an unheated garage, but did have some immediately afterward. States are generally pretty lenient in their application of the accident test.

"Arises Out of Employment"

The question here is did your injury or illness come from your job or from something else? Do you have back problems because of the daily lifting you do on the job or because of that car accident you were in a few years back? Did you develop cancer because of something you continually breathed in at work or because you smoke? These are seldom easy questions to resolve; typically, they will require expert medical testimony for a final determination.

"During the Course of Employment"

This test is similar but not identical to the previous one. To receive money from the workers' comp system, your injury or illness must have happened while you were in the line of duty. In many cases where the injury occurs on working time in a work area, this test is very easily satisfied. The machine you were using blew up and injured you "during the course of employment." Other cases are less obvious. What if you're on your way to work? What if you're on a business trip? What if you're at the company picnic or the Christmas party? These things "arise out of employment," but do they occur "during the course of employment?" There are some special rules that states generally apply to the exceptional cases. These are the most common:

The "Going and Coming" Rule Injuries suffered while commuting to and from work are usually not considered to have happened "during the course of employment." Therefore, they're not going to get you any workers' comp money. Some exceptions to this rule that are compensable include injuries that occur (1) when you're in the employer's parking lot or on the verge of going in the employer's front door, (2) when your employer has required you to drive certain cars (for example, for sales and repair jobs), (3) when you're on business travel that's reimbursed by your employer, (4) when you're being vanned-in to work by your employer, (5) when you're running an errand for your employer, and sometimes (6) when your home is your second job site. Courts will differ, though, on what's an acceptable exception to the coming and going rule.

Horseplay at Work   If you're injured while fooling around with another employee or while violating some employer's rule, you'll seldom receive workers' compensation. An exception, though, is if your employer condones your behavior (for instance, if the boss organized an impromptu game of wiffle ball in the employee lounge during a break and you tripped over the couch at second base, breaking your arm).

Picnics and Parties   If the event was held at your worksite or on paid time, or if your employer pays for the event to be held elsewhere and you're required to go, any injury you suffer at this event will likely be considered "during the course of employment." Similar standards apply if you're hurt while playing on a company ball team.

Using these four tests, let's briefly dissect the scenario that opened this chapter. Because Lisa's injury was physical, unexpected, and traceable to a definite time, place, and event, the injury passes the first two tests. Did it "arise out of employment?" Yes, because she didn't have the concussion when she went into work but she did have it afterward. How about "during the course of employment?" Again, the answer is yes, because the accident happened at work, during working time, and while she was performing her normal duties. This is an easy case. Lisa should be able to collect workers' comp benefits. But what exactly will she get?

Workers' Compensation Benefits

Workers' comp is really several types of insurance in one. First, it's medical insurance. It pays your medical bills for doctors, nurses, hospitalization, specialists, drugs, and occasionally for physical and vocational rehabilitation.

Second, it's life insurance. If you die on the job, your spouse and dependents will begin receiving workers' comp checks to replace some of the income that you would have brought home.

Third, it's disability insurance. If you survive your accident, but are temporarily or permanently disabled, after a short waiting period (usually three days to one week depending on the state) you'll receive between 50 and 70 percent of your average weekly wage (up to a maximum) for some period of time. How long depends on how severe and how permanent your injury is. The law recognizes four categories of injury:

1. An injury that permits you to still work a little and is expected to have no permanent consequences (for example, a sprain or a fracture)
2. An injury that doesn't permit you to work at all for a period of time, but is not expected to have any permanent consequences (for example, a serious illness or a concussion)
3. An injury that permits you to still work a little, but is expected to leave you with a permanent physical loss or a permanent reduction in your ability to earn money (for example, loss of an eye or a limb)
4. An injury that leaves you unable to work at all and is expected to be permanent (the types of injuries that fit this category will depend on your age, skills, education, and experience).

In most states, as the severity and permanence of the injury increase, so will the amount of time that you can collect from workers' comp. Your state workers' compensation agency can provide you with the details of your law when you file a claim.

Many states also have what's called a "schedule" of benefits written right into their workers' comp law. This schedule will say exactly how many thousands of dollars a lost body part is worth to you. Some states use this schedule to determine what you're entitled to regardless of your income. Others grant you this lump sum in addition to a weekly disability benefit.

Summary

Your workers' comp law helps you get quick compensation and medical coverage for work-related injuries. But don't expect to be seeing workers' comp recipients buying new Porsches any time soon. While workers' comp gives you some temporary security during your disability, it merely keeps you from slipping into poverty.

If you're injured on the job, immediately notify your employer and then call your state workers' compensation agency to file a claim. If that claim is challenged by your employer, it's rarely a good idea to handle the case yourself. If you have the financial resources, hire an experienced attorney. You can bet your employer is probably going to do the same.

Other Common Question about Workers' Compensation

Q: Is everybody covered by workers' comp?

A: Almost all workers are covered. Generally excluded from coverage are agricultural/farm laborers, domestic and household employees, volunteers, independent contractors, and—in some states—those who work for employers that have fewer than three employees.

State and local government employees are typically covered by a special state compensation system. Federal employees look to the Federal Employees' Compensation Act for protection. This law is administered by the Office of Workers' Compensation Programs at the U.S. Department of Labor (202-219-7503).

Q: Can my boss fire me while I'm out of work collecting workers' comp?

A: Recall from the Discrimination and Discharge section of this book that your employer usually has no obligation to keep you employed. However, you can't be terminated or laid off for discriminatory reasons. For instance, your boss can't fire you simply because you're now disabled. He or she must first comply with the provisions of the Americans with Disabilities Act (see chapter 4). Similarly, *you cannot be fired because you filed a workers' comp claim.*

Q: After I got hurt, my employer required me to see the company doctor. Is that legal?

A: Yes, but your employer has to pay for the examination. Often, employers are seeking to determine if you're really injured. Also, they're looking for ammunition to challenge your workers' comp claim. Therefore, it's always a good idea to see your own doctor as well. Both you and your employer must make all medical reports available to the other party upon request.

Q: I was just injured trimming my hedges and now I can't work for a while. Will workers' comp cover me even though my injury had nothing to do with work?

A: No, but there are five states (California, Hawaii, New Jersey, New York, and Rhode Island) that have what is called **Temporary Disability Insurance** (TDI) for workers in your situation. TDI offers a weekly check to workers who are temporarily disabled through a nonoccupational accident or illness (and sometimes to pregnant workers as well). Usually, there's a seven-day waiting period for benefits which average about half of your weekly salary (capped at approximately $300). Both you and your employer must contribute a small amount to the TDI fund (except in California, where employers don't have to contribute). Benefits last up to fifty-two weeks in California, and up to twenty-six weeks in the other four states.

Appendix A
Government Agency
Phone Numbers

Federal Agency Phone Numbers

You can also consult the blue pages of your telephone book and the *United States Government Manual* in your local library for the number of your regional office for these agencies.

Equal Employment Opportunity Commission	202-663-4900
Internal Revenue Service	800-829-1040
National Labor Relations Board	202-273-1000
Occupational Safety and Health Administration	202-219-8151
Pension and Welfare Benefits Administration	202-219-8921
Social Security Administration	800-772-1213
	410-965-7700
United States Department of Labor	202-219-6411
Wage and Hour Division	202-219-8305

Phone Numbers of State Departments

State	Labor Department	Human Rights Commission	Workers' Comp. Agency	Unemployment Agency	Occup. Safety and Health Agency
Alabama	205-242-3460	205-242-1550	205-242-8990	205-242-8025	205-254-1275
Alaska	907-465-2700	907-276-7474	907-465-2790	907-465-2712	907-465-4855
Arizona	602-542-4411	602-542-5263	602-631-2050	602-542-3667	602-255-5795
Arkansas	501-682-4500	***	501-372-3930	501-682-3201	501-682-4522
California	415-737-2600	415-557-1180	415-557-1946	916-445-9212	415-737-2959

Phone Numbers of State Departments, Continued

State	Labor Department	Human Rights Commission	Workers' Comp. Agency	Unemployment Agency	Occup. Safety and Health Agency
Colorado	303-837-3800	303-894-2997	303-764-2906	303-866-6032	***
Connecticut	203-566-4384	203-566-3350	203-789-7783	203-566-5790	203-566-4550
Delaware	302-571-2710	302-577-3485	302-571-3594	302-368-6730	302-577-3908
District of Columbia	202-576-6942	202-939-8740	202-724-0702	202-639-1163	202-576-6339
Florida	904-488-7228	904-488-7082	904-488-2514	904-488-6093	904-488-7421
Georgia	404-656-3011	404-656-1737	404-656-2034	404-656-3050	404-894-6644
Hawaii	808-548-3150	808-548-4533	808-548-5414	808-548-4064	808-548-4155
Idaho	208-334-3950	208-334-2873	208-334-6000	208-334-6466	208-334-3950
Illinois	312-782-6206	312-814-6245	312-814-6555	312-793-4240	***
Indiana	317-232-2663	317-232-2612	317-232-3809	317-232-8087	317-633-0692
Iowa	515-281-8067	515-281-4121	515-281-5934	515-281-4986	515-281-8113
Kansas	913-296-7475	913-296-3206	913-296-3441	913-296-3534	913-296-4386
Kentucky	502-564-3070	502-564-3550	502-564-5550	502-564-2990	502-564-6892
Louisiana	504-342-3011	504-342-6729	504-342-7836	504-342-3017	504-342-3126
Maine	207-289-3786	207-289-2326	207-289-3751	207-289-2316	207-289-6400
Maryland	301-333-4179	301-333-1715	301-333-4700	301-333-5306	301-333-4195
Massachusetts	617-727-3455	617-727-3990	617-727-4900	617-727-6638	617-727-3567
Michigan	517-322-1289	517-335-3165	517-322-1296	313-876-5467	517-335-9218
Minnesota	612-296-2342	612-296-5665	612-296-6490	612-296-3711	612-296-4532
Mississippi	601-354-8711	601-359-1406	601-987-4200	601-961-7700	601-987-3981
Missouri	314-751-4091	314-751-3325	314-751-4231	314-751-3641	314-751-3403
Montana	406-444-3555	406-444-2884	406-444-7794	406-444-2723	406-444-3671
Nebraska	402-475-2934	402-471-2024	402-471-2568	402-471-9000	402-471-2239
Nevada	702-687-4850	702-486-7161	702-687-5284	702-687-4510	702-687-5240
New Hampshire	603-271-3171	603-271-2767	603-271-3172	603-224-3311	603-271-2024
New Jersey	609-292-2323	201-648-2700	609-232-2414	609-292-2460	609-292-2313
New Mexico	505-827-6875	505-827-6838	505-841-8787	505-841-8431	505-827-2888
New York	518-457-2741	212-870-8790	718-802-6700	518-457-2177	518-457-3518
North Carolina	919-733-7166	919-733-7996	919-733-4820	919-733-7883	919-733-3589
North Dakota	701-224-2661	701-224-2661	701-224-2700	701-224-2833	701-221-5188
Ohio	614-644-2223	614-466-2785	614-466-1935	614-466-9755	614-466-3564
Oklahoma	405-521-2461	405-521-3441	405-557-7600	405-557-7218	405-528-1500
Oregon	503-229-5737	503-229-6600	503-378-3308	503-378-3214	503-378-3272
Pennsylvania	717-787-3756	717-787-4410	717-653-4428	717-787-5122	717-787-3323
Rhode Island	401-277-2741	401-277-2661	401-272-0700	401-277-3649	401-457-1800
South Carolina	803-734-9603	803-2536336	803-737-9450	803-737-2787	803-734-9644
South Dakota	605-773-3101	605-773-4493	605-773-3681	605-622-2452	***
Tennessee	615-741-2582	615-741-5825	615-741-2793	615-741-3178	615-741-2793
Texas	512-463-3172	512-450-3030	512-322-3490	512-463-2661	512-459-1611
Utah	801-530-6921	801-530-6921	801-530-6880	801-533-2201	801-530-6901
Vermont	802-828-2286	802-828-3171	802-223-7226	802-229-0311	802-828-2286
Virginia	804-786-2377	804-662-9971	804-367-8615	804-786-3004	804-786-2391
Washington	206-753-6307	206-753-6770	206-753-6376	206-753-5120	206-753-6500
West Virginia	304-348-7890	304-348-2616	304-348-0475	304-348-2624	304-348-3526
Wisconsin	608-266-7552	608-266-0946	608-226-1340	608-266-7074	608-266-1816
Wyoming	307-777-7261	307-777-6381	307-777-7441	307-235-3200	307-777-7786

Note: These numbers change frequently, so consult your telephone book if necessary.

Appendix B
Important Statutes and Cases

For More Information

For those readers who want to investigate specific employment rights more deeply, this appendix offers guidance about where to find information. Listed below are the most important statutes and cases that have shaped the boundaries of your rights on the job. Of course, the case list is not comprehensive, but it is included to provide a sampling of the many relevant cases in employment law.

Finding Information

You should be able to find the complete text of the federal statutes and most of your state's employment statutes in any university library. Also, larger local libraries should have these statutes as well.

To find the cases, however, you may have to visit a law library at either a university or your county court house. Don't worry about the confusing numbers and letters following the case names. These are the case *citations*. The first number is the book volume, the letters following it tell you what court decided the case, and the number following the letters notes the page on which the case begins. The number in parentheses is the year the case was decided. So *411 US 792 (1973)* refers you to a case decided by the U.S. Supreme

Court in 1973; the court's opinion is recorded in volume 411 of "United States Reports," page 792. The citations below that do not say include "U.S." refer you to cases decided by courts other than the United States Supreme Court.

However, **you do not need to know how to use these citations or how to find a case.** Every law library has a reference librarian to assist you. If you show him or her the citation, he or she will show you where the case is located. But be prepared. Those of you who have never read a court decision before may find them frustrating and tiresome. They tend to be long, wordy, and very legalistic.

One alternative to this may be to find an employment law textbook in a university library. These texts include the most important cases in employment law and include court opinions that have been edited to focus on the relevant parts. They also include notes after each case to refer you to other cases on the same subject. Use of employment law texts might be a more efficient and less painful way for you to conduct further research.

Finally, the various departments and agencies discussed in this book and listed in Appendix A offer advice and packets of information free of charge to those who request them. This may be the most efficient method of all for getting your questions answered.

Federal Statutes

National Labor Relations Act (1935)
Fair Labor Standards Act (1938)
Equal Pay Act (1963)
Civil Rights Act of 1964, Title VII
Age Discrimination in Employment Act (1967)
Occupational Safety and Health Act (1970)
Employee Retirement Income and Security Act (1974)
Pregnancy Discrimination Act (1978)
Consolidated Omnibus Budget Reconciliation Act (1985)
Immigration Reform and Control Act (1986)
Employee Polygraph Protection Act (1988)
Worker Adjustment and Retraining Notification Act
  (1988)
Americans with Disabilities Act (1990)

Civil Rights Act of 1991
Family and Medical Leave Act (1993)

Court Cases

I. Discrimination Law: Race and Sex

Disparate treatment: *McDonnell Douglass Corp. v. Green, 411 US 792 (1973)*

Disparate impact: *Griggs v. Duke Power Co., 401 US 424 (1971); Albemarle Paper Co. v. Moody, 422 US 425 (1975)*

Bona fide occupational qualification: *Diaz v. Pan American World Airways, 442 F.2d 385 (5th Circuit, 1971); Dothard v. Rawlinson, 433 US 321 (1977); United Auto Workers v. Johnson Controls Inc. 111 S.Ct 1196 (1991)*

Affirmative action: *United Steelworkers of America v. Weber, 443 US 193 (1979); Johnson v. Transportation Agency, Santa Clara County, 480 US 616 (1987)*

Sexual harassment: *Harris v. Forklift Systems, US (1993); Meritor Savings Bank v. Vinson, 477 US 57 (1986); Ellison v. Brady, 924 F.2d 872 (9th Circuit, 1991)*

II. Other Discrimination Law

Religious discrimination: *Trans World Airlines v. Hardison, 432 US 63 (1977)*

National origin discrimination: *Espinoza v. Farah Manufacturing Co., 414 US 86 (1973)*

Age discrimination: *Western Air Lines v. Criswell, 472 US 400 (1985)*

Disability discrimination: *School Board of Nassau County, Florida v. Arline, 480 US 273 (1987)*

III. Common Law Exceptions to Employment-at-will

Employment-at-will doctrine defined: *Payne v. Western and Atlantic Railroad, 81 Tenn 507 (Tennessee Supreme Court 1884)*

Examples of personnel policy manuals as contracts: *Toussaint v. Blue Cross & Blue Shield of Michigan, 292 NW 2d 880 (Michigan Supreme Court 1980); Woolley v. Hoffman LaRouche, 491 A.2d 1257 (New Jersey Supreme Court 1985)*

Examples of public policy exceptions: *Nees v. Hock 536 P.2d 512 (Oregon Supreme Court 1975); Brunner v. Al Attar, 786 SW 2d 784 (Texas Court of Appeals 1990)*

Examples of the implied covenant of good faith and fair dealing: *Rulon-Miller v. International Business Machines Corp., 162 Cal.App.3d 241 (California Court of Appeals 1984); Stark v. Circle K Corp., 751 P.2d 162 (Montana Supreme Court 1988)*

IV Employee Privacy

Employee searches: *K-Mart Corp. v. Trotti, 677 SW 2d 632 (Texas Court of Appeals 1984)*

Employee monitoring: *McLain v. Boise Cascade Corp., 533 P.2d 343 (Oregon Supreme Court, 1975)*

Drug testing: *National Treasury Employees Union v. Von Raab, 489 US 656 (1989); Skinner v. Railway Labor Executives Association, 489 US 602 (1989)*

V. Unions and Management (Labor Law)

Duty of fair representation: *Ford Motor Company v. Huffman, 345 US 330 (1953); Vaca v. Sipes 386 US 171 (1967); Hines v. Anchor Motor Freight, 424 US 554 (1976)*

Firing strikers: *NLRB v. Mackay Radio and Telegraph Co., 304 US 333 (1938)*

Employer conduct before the election: *Midland National Life Insurance Co., 263 NLRB 127 (1982); NLRB v. Gissel Packing Co., 395 US 575 (1969)*

Union representation when being disciplined: *NLRB v. Weingarten, Inc., 420 US 251 (1975)*

Nonmembers objecting to paying union dues: *Communications Workers of America v. Beck, 487 US 735 (1988)*

VI. Other Issues

Validity of a minimum wage law: *West Coast Hotel Co. v. Parrish, 300 US 379 (1937)*

Who must participate in Social Security: *United States v. Lee, 455 US 252 (1982)*

OSHA inspections: *Marshall v. Barlow's Inc., 436 US 307 (1978); Whirlpool Corp. v. Marshall, 445 US 1 (1980)*

Index